Memoirs of Mrs. William Veitch, Mr. Thomas Hog of Kiltearn, Mr. Henry Erskine and Mr. John Carstairs;

Free Church of Scotland. General Assembly, Marion Fairly Veitch

15/-

MEMOIRS

OF

MRS WILLIAM VEITCH,

MR THOMAS HOG OF KILTEARN,

MR HENRY ERSKINE,

AND

MR JOHN CARSTAIRS.

ISSUED BY THE COMMITTEE OF
THE GENERAL ASSEMBLY OF THE FREE CHURCH OF SCOTLAND
FOR THE PUBLICATION OF THE WORKS OF
SCOTTISH REFORMERS AND DIVINES.

EDINBURGH:
PRINTED FOR THE ASSEMBLY'S COMMITTEE.
MDCCCXLVI.

EDINBURGH:
PRINTED BY JOHN GREIG.

INTRODUCTION.

BY THE EDITOR.

Our plan of publication, it will be recollected, comprised not merely the sermons and doctrinal writings of the illustrious Fathers of our church, but also, the Memoirs of these men, as well as those Histories in which the dealings of God with regard to the progress of our church in general are recorded. In this manner, it was hoped, that the useful would be blended with the agreeable, and narrative with doctrine, so that every variety of taste in reading might be successively gratified. In conformity with this intention, the present volume of Biography has been produced, which will be followed from time to time by others of a similar description, as well as those of a more ample and detailed character, in which a complete portraiture is given of those distinguished men whose piety and usefulness were so eminent, and whose course was so filled with trials and vicissitudes.

In the present supplementary volume of the first year, four short Memoirs have been given, the first of which is that of Mrs Veitch, written by herself, and hitherto unpublished. This excellent woman, who endured an amount of domestic affliction and vexatious persecution, in many cases more trying than martyrdom itself, was most deservedly esteemed and honoured by the pious and distinguished of her own day; and such was the estimation in which her prudence and sound sense were held, that she was frequently called by her husband and other persecuted ministers, to the counsels they held under the most perplexing emergencies. With all this, her more than feminine, her truly Christian gentleness is so conspicuous, that the readers of her memoir will be struck with the silence in which she passes over most of her sufferings, as well as the dispassionate and forgiving tone in which she alludes to those by whom they were inflicted. To understand these more thoroughly, we would recommend to our readers the perusal of the Life of her husband, the Rev. William Veitch of Dumfries, either that which has been edited by Dr M'Crie, or that which is more briefly contained in the Scots Worthies. Of the value attached to her Diary, we quote the following extract from the first of these works. She (Mrs Veitch) " proved a wife of eminent piety, as several instances after narrated, and a manuscript of her own would testify, which I once did see; and it contains as strange actings of faith upon the word of God, answers of prayer, and revelations of the mind of God, as peradventure the age she lived in can parallel; and that, both with respect to the public work of God, and also her husband and family's case under their long and great sufferings, will abundantly evince."

From the tone and spirit of the Diary, it is evident, that, so far from being intended for publication, it was designed to be merely a private memento for herself, and afterwards a bequest for the instruction of her children. We are happy in being the means of giving its usefulness a wider range than ever its amiable writer could have contemplated. Three copies only exist in manuscript of the Diary, from one of which, belonging to the Rev. George Panton, of Heriot's Hospital (for whose kindness on this occasion, the Committee return their warmest thanks), the present imprint has been taken. A few notes added by the writer of this short preface, will explain some of those passing circumstances which are briefly adverted to in the original.

Of the second Life of this series—that of Hog of Kiltearn—it is unnecessary here to speak, as anything connected with its republication, of any importance, is sufficiently explained in the chapter prefixed to it. The third, which is the Life of Mr Henry Erskine, has been extracted from a manuscript in the Advocates' Library; but by which of his sons it was written, whether by Ralph or Ebenezer, or whether it is the original manuscript, or a copy from the original, we find ourselves incompetent to decide. The fourth, which contains but a few particulars in the life of John Carstairs, is from the pen of the indefatigable Wodrow.

In conclusion, we are happy to announce, that a long and interesting array of History and Biography stretches before us, much of which has not yet seen the light, or has been published but partially, and in a mutilated form. To this, we hope to have the pleasure of introducing our readers, as speedily as our system of publication will permit.

MEMOIRS

OF THE

LIFE OF MRS VEITCH.

MEMOIRS

OF THE

LIFE OF MRS VEITCH,

SPOUSE TO THE REV. MR WILLIAM VEITCH, MINISTER OF THE GOSPEL AT DUMFRIES.

AN ACCOUNT OF THE LORD'S GRACIOUS DEALING WITH ME; AND OF HIS REMARKABLE HEARING AND ANSWERING MY SUPPLICATIONS.

IT pleased God, of his great goodness, early to incline my heart to seek him, and bless him that I was born in a land where the gospel was at that time purely and powerfully preached; as also, that I was born of godly parents, and well educated. But above all things, I bless him that he made me see, that nothing but the righteousness of Christ could save me from the wrath of God.

One day, having been at prayer, and coming into the room, where one was reading a letter of Mr Rutherford's (then only in manuscript), directed to one John Gordon of Risco,—giving an account how far one might go, and yet prove a hypocrite and miss heaven, — it occasioned great exercise to me. Misbelief said, I should go to hell; but one day at prayer, the Lord was graciously pleased to set home upon my heart that word, "To whom, Lord, shall

A

we go ? thou hast the words of eternal life," (John vi. 68).
And at another time, that word, "Those that seek me
early shall find me," (Prov. viii. 17). And at another
time, that word, " For my thoughts are not your thoughts,"
&c. (Isa. lv. 8). And at another time, that word, " The
Lord taketh pleasure in them that fear him, in those that
hope in his mercy," (Psal. cxlvii. 11), which was very refreshing to me.

Some years after, when providence seemed to call me to
change my lot, because many suitors came, it was often my earnest supplication to the Lord, that I might be matched in him,
and for his glory, which graciously he was pleased to grant
me. Yet in this business I met with difficulties; several of
my friends dissuading me from it by diverse reasons, and
this among others, that it was an ill time, and I might be
brought to straits in the world,* which bred much trouble
to my spirit, and put me many a time to seek His mind in
it. At length He set home that word, " Our fathers trusted
in thee, and thou didst deliver them," (Psal. xxii. 4); and,
" They trusted in thee and were not confounded," (verse 5).
Upon this I was inclined to trust Him, both for spirituals
and temporals; and these promises were remarkably made
good to me in all the various places of my sojourning in
diverse kingdoms, which I here mention to the commendation of his faithfulness. His word in this has been a tried
word to me, worthy to be recorded, to encourage me to
trust him for the future; who heretofore has not only provided well for me and mine, but made me, in the places
where my lot was cast, useful to others, and made that
word good, " As having nothing, and yet possessing all
things," (2 Cor. vi. 10).

A little after I was married, the storm of persecution

---

* The maiden name of Mrs Veitch was Marion Fairly; the place of
her residence was Lanark. Her marriage occurred on November 23,
1664, a period when Presbyterianism was overturned in Scotland, and
many of the faithful pastors and teachers ejected; among others, her
own husband, who had been Chaplain to Sir Hugh Campbell of Calder.

arose upon us, to the parting of my husband and me, and increased so, as I was necessitated to leave my native land.*

Having borne four children before I came out of Scotland, two of them died in the land, the other two I brought with me; and being deprived of what once I had there, I renewed my suit to God for me and mine, and that was, that he would give us the tribe of Levi's inheritance, "For the Lord God was their inheritance," (Josh. xiii. 33). When I entered into a strange land, I besought the Lord that he would give me food to eat, and raiment to put on, and bring me back to see his glory in Scotland. This promise was exactly made out to me.

Several years after, it pleased the Lord to let my husband fall into the enemy's hands, who took him, January 19th, 1679, about five o'clock in the morning, in Stantonhall, which bred some trouble, and new fear to my spirit; but he was graciously pleased to set home that word, "He does all things well," (Mark vii. 37); "Trust in the Lord, and fear not what man can do," (Psal. lvi. 11); which brought peace to me in such a measure, that I was made often to wonder; for all the time the officers were in the house, He supported me, so that I was not in the least discouraged before them, which made Major Oglethorpe say, he wondered to see me. I told him, I looked to a higher hand than his in this, and I knew he could not go one hair-breadth beyond God's permission. He answered, that He permits his enemies to go a great length sometimes. They took him to prison, where he lay about twelve days. All this time I was under much exercise of spirit, which made me go to God many times on his behalf. He made that word often sweet to me, "He performeth the things appointed for me," (Job xxiii. 14); and that, "He is of one mind, and who can turn him?" (ver. 13). Much means were used for his

---

* Mr Veitch was obliged to fly to England, in consequence of having joined that body of Covenanters who were routed at Pentland Hills. After several dangers and changes, he settled in the parish of Rothbury in Northumberland, where his wife and family rejoined him in 1671.

liberty, but all to no effect, which bred new errands to God for him and me. But misbelief coming in, and telling many ill tales of God, was like to discourage me; to wit, that I was a stranger in a strange land, and had six small children, and little in the world to look to: But he comforted me with these words :—

> "O why art thou cast down, my soul;
> What should discourage thee?
> And why with vexing thoughts art thou
> Disquieted in me?

Still trust in him, for I shall yet have good cause to praise him," (Psal. xliii. 5).

At length he helped me to give him freely to Him, to do with him as He pleased ; and if his blood should fill up the cup of the enemy, and bring about deliverance to His Church, I would betake myself to his care and providence for me and my children : And while I was yet speaking to God in prayer, that word was wonderfully brought into my mind, " Abraham, hold thy hand, for I have provided a sacrifice," (Gen. xxii. 11, 12), which comforted me concerning my husband ; and that word, " The meal in the barrel shall not waste, nor the oil in the cruise, until the Lord send rain on the earth," (1 Kings xvii. 14), which brought much peace to my troubled spirit concerning my family. I thought I had now ground to believe he should not die ; but misbelief soon got the upper hand, and told me, it was not the language of faith, which put me to go to God, and pour out my spirit before him. And He answered me with that word, " They that walk in darkness, and have no light, let them trust in the Lord, and stay themselves on their God," (Isa. l. 10), which refreshed me much, and gave me more ground to believe he should not die. He wrote to me in the night, that there was an order from the king to remove him to Edinburgh. When I opened the letter, he had that expression, " Deep calleth unto deep," &c. But He was pleased to set home that word, " Good is the word of the Lord," which silenced much my misbelief. I rode along with the man that night, but could get no access until the morning. When I came in, the soldiers were guarding him;

but the kettle-drums beating the troops presently to arms, we were soon parted, and he carried out to the streets, and set on horse-back among the ranks, the town's people running to gaze. All these things were against me, and conspired to frighten me; but that word being set home, wonderfully supported me, "Fear thou not the fear of man, but let the Lord be your fear and your dread," (Isa. viii. 12, 13). I went after to a friend's house in the town, and wept my fill, and some friends with me.

He desired that a day might be kept,* which was done in several places of the country. I went home to my children, having one upon the breast. I was under much exercise about him, and it was my suit to Him, who, I can say, is a present help in the time of trouble, that he might be keeped from the evil of sin; which he was graciously pleased to answer. Faith brought me always good news; but when misbelief was master of the field, it had never a good tale to tell of God, which often put me to review the promises; so that I may say, "Unless his laws had been my delight, I had perished in mine affliction."

A month after, he sent for me. I went in a great storm, but He strengthened me to bear that trial among many others; and that word was sweet to me, "He numbers all my wanderings." When I came, there was great hope of his freedom; but within a few days he was put in close prison, and an order came to try him for his life, which raised a new storm in me to a great height, because His providence seemed to contradict his promise; but faith brought me good news, that He would be as good as his word, but withal told me, they that believe must not make haste. Also that scripture, "Hitherto he hath helped me," and that, "Everybody seeks the ruler's favour, but every man's judgment is from the Lord," were sweet to me in that strait.

After a few months' prisoning, my good God was pleased to give orders for his liberty.† When the news came to

* For offering up prayers in his behalf.

† He was tried before the Privy Council at Edinburgh and the sen-

my ears, that word came in my mind, "He hath both spoken it, and himself hath done it; I will walk softly in the bitterness of my spirit all my days," (Isa. xxxviii. 15). We came both home in peace to our children, where we lived at Stantonhall, three miles from Morpeth, in Northumberland, August 1680.

Now, when I began to consider how He had heard me in many particulars, he inclined my heart to go to him, and seek two great suits from him. I took along these two promises: "Whatsoever thing ye desire when ye pray, believing, ye shall receive it," (Mark xi. 24). The other was that,—"Then shall ye call upon me, and ye shall go and pray unto me, and I will hearken unto you," (Jer. xxix. 12). The first suit was, eternal life to me and mine, and He helped me to believe that he was able and willing to grant that to me, as Ahasuerus was the life of Hester. It was backed also with that word, "Be it unto thee according to thy faith," which was no small comfort to me.

The other suit was, that he would return in his glory to his Church, especially to Scotland; and I had that scripture given in, "I will see their ways and heal them, and restore comfort to Zion and her mourners," (Isa. lvii. 18). Upon this, He inclined me to come often with that prayer, "Remember the word unto thy servant, upon which thou hast caused me to hope," (Psa. cxix. 49).

Within a little time a new storm arose, and my husband was again necessitated to leave me, when I had lain in of a child but about eight days; upon which I fell under great exercise of mind. Misbelief and an ill heart got the mastery of me too much, and told me, "To which of the saints wilt thou turn?" Thy not improving of the precious offers of the gospel makes God to be angry with thee, and thy husband to be removed from thee, for there is none in thy station in the country but their husbands stay with them;

tence of death, which was pronounced against him in 1666, was intended to be executed; but at the intercession of influential friends, it was changed into banishment from Scotland.

which put me many a time to pour out my spirit before Him, both in the night and day; and he was graciously pleased at length to answer me with that word, "Whom the Lord loveth he chasteneth, and scourgeth every son whom he receiveth," (Heb. xii. 6). And that word (which was sweeter to me than ever meat or drink was), "For in that he himself hath suffered, being tempted, he is able to succour them that are tempted," (Heb. ii. 17, 18). And therefore, Oh the blessed condescendency of our precious Redeemer, and the wonderful necessity he laid himself under! "In all things it behoved him to be made like unto his brethren, that he might be a merciful and faithful High Priest in things pertaining to God, to make reconciliation for the sins of the people; therefore we may come boldly unto the throne of grace, to seek grace to help in the time of need," (ver. 17). By these I got the mastery of misbelief.

My husband, some weeks after, sent me word what proffers he had for Carolina,* and he thought I might make for going thither, which bred a new exercise to me. I thought, in my old days I could have no heart for such a voyage, and leave these covenanted lands; but at length I got submission to my God, and was content, if he had more service for me and mine in another land; for I had opened my mouth and given me and mine to him and his service, when and where, and what way he pleased, and I could not go back; but if I went there, I would hang my harp upon the willows when I remembered Scotland. I made it my errand to Him, to know if I should go or not, and he was pleased to bear in that word, in prayer, upon my heart, "Though the fig-tree do not blossom," &c. (Hab. iii. 17, 18); and that, "When they persecute you in one place, flee to another, for verily I say unto you, you shall not have gone over the cities of Israel till the Son of Man be come," (Matt. x.

* This was a scheme of Sir John Cochrane and several of his associates, to emigrate to Carolina, and cultivate plantations. Their meetings were misrepresented as a plot against the government.

23). Upon which, I hoped I should not go thither, being from
that scripture persuaded that these lands in covenant with
God were the cities of Israel, which I should not go through
till deliverance came to the Church; and my husband, after
half a year's absence, came home, and staid a pretty while.

But not long after, a new storm arose, for the Justice of
the peace came to take my husband, who very narrowly escaped, and went beyond sea.*   I was lying sick in the
mean time, but in a short while I recovered.   I sent my two
eldest sons to him.   While they were at sea, there arose a
great storm, whereby many were lost.   Fear and misbelief
told me they were gone, which put me to pour out my spirit before Him.   It was my request that He would not suffer the prince of the power of the air to get his will of
them; and that word was given unto me, " He hath laid
help upon one that is mighty," (Psa. lxxxix. 19), which
gave me hope that they should not be lost, which he made
out to me, for with much difficulty they got safe to land.

Then the landlord where I dwelt came and told me, I
should stay no longer there than the term, which begat me
a new trouble, and gave me a new errand to God, for he
has appointed me to acknowledge him in all my ways, and
he would direct my steps; and that I should be careful in
nothing, but by prayer and supplication make my request
known to him, (Prov. iii. 6, and Philip. iv. 6).

My third son was dying, and he seemed not to lay death
to heart, as I would have had him, which put me many times
to pour out my heart before the Lord, for I had some
grounds to believe that he had accepted of me and mine
to be his; yet I thought the boy's practice seemed to contradict the Lord's promise to me.   This put me to beg of
Him that he would take his heart off this world, and let him
see a sight of that fair inheritance, and give him the hope
and assurance of it; and I cannot but observe how exact

* He had assisted the Marquis of Argyle in escaping to Holland, in
consequence of which he had incurred the resentment of Government.
Veitch, on this occasion, repaired soon after to the same country.

the answer was to my desires, for one day, after he called me to the bed-side, he told me he had lost conceit of the world. I asked his reason, seeing he had formerly still a desire to live. "But," said he, "and I have seen another sight." I asked what it was. He said, "I have been praying, and giving myself to Christ, and he answered me, that he took pleasure in my soul, which has comforted me." Afterwards, he said, "Is it not a wonder that Jesus Christ should have died for sinners? Oh, that is a good tale, and we should think often on it!" He had often that exclamation, "Whom have I in heaven but thee, and whom desire I in the earth besides thee?" (Psa. lxxiii. 25); which refreshed me more than he had been made heir of a great estate. After this, he desired not to be out of a heavenly discourse, or either to pray himself or to hear others pray. I thought it much from one of twelve years of age; and when he could not speak, he held up his hand when I spake to him of death and heaven. At last he put up his own hand, and closed his own eyes, and so we parted, in hope of a glorious meeting. One thing I cannot but set down, that when he was at prayer, a little before he died,—his father being absent, and his two elder brothers gone to sea,—he prayed for them all, and that his brethren and sisters might be spirited for serving God in their generation, and had that expression, "Though we be far parted now, I hope we shall meet in glory." Also, he called for his brother and sisters, and blessed them all, and bade them farewell.

All this time I was much troubled that I could not hear from my husband, because I was to remove, and would have known his mind in it, being in confusion, fear, and doubting what to do; Providence seemed to threaten us with various strokes. I went and poured out my complaint to Him, and that word was set home on my heart, "No plague shall come nigh thy dwelling, nor evil befall thee; he shall give his angels charge over thee, to keep thee in all thy ways," (Psa. xci. 10); and that word, "All things are yours, and ye are Christ's, and Christ is God's,'

(1 Cor. iii. 21). Misbelief said they were too great promises for me, but necessity made me take hold of them.

About this time, one coming to visit me, told me what Mr Carstairs had done,* and of Jerviswood's death, which raised such a trouble in my spirit, that I was scarce ever in the like; and though I had many tokens of the Lord's former hearing me, yet all that would not do, until he gave me new promises of his love to me and mine, which I hope to hold by as long as I live. I went and earnestly begged of him, that I and mine might be kept from the evil of sin, and none that waited on him might be ashamed for our sake; and he was graciously pleased to set home that word, "I will never fail thee nor forsake thee," (Heb. xiii. 5), which much refreshed me. But within a little, misbelief got the mastery of me, and it told me I need not expect to see good days. This was occasioned by the apostasy of some, and the persecutors being permitted to run all down before them, as it were. I could sleep little or none for several nights; but that word being brought home to my heart, quieted me much,—"Wo to the earth, and to the inhabitants of it, for the devil is come down with great wrath, but his time is short," (Rev. xii. 12). Then I thought what would become of the Church and his glory. In the midst of my perplexed thoughts, faith brought that word, " Be still, and know that I am God : I will be exalted among the heathen," (Psal. xlvi. 10); and, "When they flourish as the grass, it is that they may be destroyed for ever," (Psal. xcii. 7); and they are but set in slippery places ; their feet shall slide in due time, (Deut. xxxii. 35).

But fear and misbelief said, He would not return with his glory to Scotland, and I should not see it, "and thy sins are the cause ;" which puzzled me that I could not sleep.

* Carstairs was tried as an agent in the Ryehouse plot, and tortured with the thumbkins, but would confess nothing. At length, on being threatened with the boots, he yielded, upon condition that government should make no use of his confessions against any one. But the judges shamefully violated this pledge, and made use of his confessions in the condemnation of Baillie of Jerviswood.

But faith told me, that the King of our Israel was a merciful King; if I would come with a rope about my neck, he would not put me away. And "although my house be not so with God, yet he hath made with me an everlasting covenant, ordered in all things, and sure," (2 Sam. xxiii. 5), which not a little comforted me.

But when I began to consult with carnal reason, it told me there was no hope. And one night I was offering up my desires to him for the Church of Scotland, that word was set home to me, " Thine eyes shall see thy teachers," (Isa. xxx. 20); and that,—" Thy life shall be given thee for a prey in all places," &c. (Jer. xlv. 5); and that,—"Thy bread shall be given thee, and thy water shall be sure," (Isa. xxxiii. 16); and that word, " Fear not, for they that be with us are more than they that be with them," (2 Kings vi. 16), which gave me some ground to believe, that yet it should be well with the Church.

Not long after, one came in and told me, my schoolmaster was taken at Newcastle (being there about some business), and they feared he might be sent into Scotland, and put in the boots; and likewise, that they were afraid the Justices might come and search my house. This occasioned great trouble, it happening at such a time as is last mentioned, my husband absent, &c. This made me many a time go to His door, and cry for help; and that word was often brought to my mind, " Why art thou afraid of a man that shall die, and of the son of man, that shall be made as grass, and forgettest the Lord thy Maker?" (Isa. li. 12, 13): " He hath delivered in six troubles, and in seven he will not fail thee or forsake thee," (Job v. 19). His faithfulness shall be a shield and buckler unto thee. Yet fear and misbelief said there was no hope, which made me have many a perplexed day and night.

Another time, when I was much puzzled what would become of the Church, especially Scotland, that word was brought to my mind, " Thou shalt decree a thing, and it shall be established," (Job xxii. 28), which I thought was a strange word. I went to God with it, and told him, that which he inclined me to decree, was eternal life to me and mine, and that we might be kept from the evil of sin; and that he would return in his glory to Scotland, and that mine might be useful to him, and that if it was his good pleasure I might see it; and if he had no pleasure in me, let him do with me as he pleased. And while I was offering up my desires in prayer to him, that word was brought to my mind, "Be it unto thee as thou wilt," (Matt. xv. 28). When I began to consider on it, I thought it was as strange a word as ever I met with. Carnal reason and misbelief said, it was impossible that ever I should obtain that which was a new errand for me to Him. And while I was thus perplexed with strange thoughts, that word was given in to me, "I am the God of all flesh: is there any thing too hard for me?" (Jer. xxxii. 27), which gave misbelief a great stroke; but within a little, it got up on me again, for word came that there was no hope of the godly man, our schoolmaster's getting free, and that he would be sent away to Edinburgh, which made me go to God for him; for in the day of my strait, and while my children were like sheep without a shepherd, it was my desire to God, that he would provide one for them: which wonderfully he did, and brought him to me, without ever seeking him; which made me beg God many a time, that he might not be used the worse for me and mine's sake. Then was that word set home, "He has delivered, and he will deliver," (2 Cor. i. 10), which I thought gave me ground to believe it should be well with him; and about a month after he was set at liberty, which, when I had heard, that word came in, "Happy is the man that hath the God of Jacob for his help, and whose hope is in the Lord," which I have good reason to say, for he never disappointed me; yet such is the baseness of my deceitful heart, that whenever I meet with a new trouble, I have my faith a seeking.

I could not hear from my husband, and the time of flitting was near. Misbelief and an ill heart were ready to tell me, that people would fear to give me a house; but that word was brought to my mind, "Trust in him at all times, thou knowest not what a day might bring forth," (Psal. lxii. 8).

One day, I was much troubled with misbelief and an ill heart. I went to prayer to God that he would rebuke them, and I thought I got not that help from him which sometimes I had got: but he inclined my heart to go to his word, which had been my counsellor in all my doubts and fears; and the first place that offered to me was, "Count it all joy when ye fall into diverse temptations," (James i. 2); and that word upon the back of it, "Jehovah hear thee in the day of trouble: the name of the God of Jacob defend thee, send thee help from the sanctuary, and strengthen thee out of Zion," (Psal. xx. 1, 2), which was sweet to me.

At length I heard that my husband was well, by a letter that my son had written to one in Newcastle; but when I heard the person had a letter from Holland, telling that he was well, which was intercepted, (and Sir Thomas Armstrong was taken in Holland, and brought to London and hanged*), which made me fear he had written another back to him with the post, it much troubled me, thinking that might be a mean of taking him. All the former experiences of God's goodness to me could not silence my misbelief; I went and poured out my spirit in prayer before Him, who answered me with that word, "He shall not die, but live, and declare the works of the Lord," (Psal. cxviii. 17), which gave me ground of hope, till carnal fear and misbelief said he would be taken. But another time, when I was pleading with God for him, that he might be spared, and useful for him; for I thought he might have some service for him, seeing he had so wonderfully preserved him, after I had given him freely to him; and he was graciously pleased to set home that word, "I change not, and he shall not be consumed," (Mal. iii. 6), which made me to wonder, and see that his Spirit backing his word, is like the tree cast

---

* This was on the charge of having been engaged in the Ryehouse Plot.

into the waters of affliction, it makes them sweet; and it
pleased him to send the person who had written this letter
to my house, who gave me full satisfaction that there was
no hazard upon that account.

Soon after, word came that the king was dead. When
I heard it, I thought Pharaoh was dead, and I would go to
God, and beg of him, that he would spirit a Moses to lead
forth the Church from under her hard bondage; and that
word was put in my mind, " O Israel, return unto me, for
thou hast fallen by thine iniquity. Take with you words,
and turn to the Lord," &c., (Hos. xiv. 1, 2). And I pled
with him at another time, that the people of his holiness
had possessed it but a little while, and that our adversaries
had trodden down the sanctuary, (Isa. lxiii. 18) ; and that I
had heard with mine ears what great things he had done
for our fathers, (Psal. xliv. 1). He set home that word,
" I change not, and they shall not be consumed," (Mal. iii.
6). And that *   *   * which made me hope he would not
leave these covenanted lands, especially Scotland. And
yet unbelief would say, There is no hope. Another time
that word was brought in my mind, " This is the confidence
which we have in him, if we ask any thing according to his
will, he heareth us," (1 John v. 14). Upon which I begged
that he would return in his glory, and build his Church ;
and I had that word, " Not for your sakes will I do this,
but for my own name's sake," (Ezek. xxxvi. 22), which
gave me ground to believe that he would get help.

Now the term of my removing was come. I went about
fifteen miles from Stantonhall, which is in Northumberland, where I had lived eight years, to Newcastle, anno
1684; where I was not well settled, when Argyle and
Monmouth had appeared, which bred much trouble in the
place : and it put me to plead, that He would remember the
word upon which he had caused me to hope, to wit, that
promise, " No plague shall near thy dwelling come," (Psal.
xci.) ; and I may say he made it visibly out to me at that
time, for though there was much trouble round about me,

yet no evil befel my dwelling.   Then it was my desire, that
He would make good his word on which He had caused me
to hope in behalf of the Church; for I thought possibly
this might be the time of building his house.   But his
thoughts are not like mine; for it pleased him, who gives
no account of his matters, to let both these great persons
fall before the enemy, which put me to pour out my spirit
before him, and often to charge my soul to be silent, for my
ill heart and misbelief were like to quarrel with him.   Oh,
what a great difficulty is it to trust and believe in him, when
his providences seem to contradict his promises !   But when
faith is master of the house, it will read love in his heart,
when he strikes with his hand.   Under my great pressure
of spirit, and despondency at this time, he set home that
word, "The vision is for an appointed time, but at the
end it shall speak, and not lie : though it tarry, wait for it ;
because it will surely come," (Hab. ii. 3), which was very
sweet to me, and silenced misbelief very much.   But within
a little, carnal reason and an ill heart said there was no
hope that He would return to his covenanted people in
these lands; and that I should not see that which I had
some ground to believe from his word that I should see.
And one time when I was offering up my desires, that he
would give me grace and strength to master misbelief, he
was graciously pleased to set home that word, "And thou
shalt know that I am the Lord, for they shall not be
ashamed that wait on me," (Isa. xlix. 23), which was refreshing to me, and made me to say, "What am I, or my
father's house," (1 Chron. xvii. 16), that free love should
condescend to such a piece of sinful clay ?   But I see free
love is above reason.   Misbelief got a great stroke with this
promise.

A little after, when I began to take a look of what He
had given me ground, as I thought, to see, and how unlike
it was to be performed, misbelief again was like to prevail,
and I went to Him, who had many a time helped me, and
never disappointed me in any thing he promised; and he

was graciously pleased to bring that word to me, " Though ye believe not, yet he abideth faithful, and cannot deny himself," (2 Tim. ii. 13), which quieted my mind, so that I may say from many experiences, he is a present help in the time of trouble. And as to the riches that lie in the word, the promises, ordinances, and duties, rightly read, rightly pleaded, and rightly discharged, I may say as the Queen of Sheba, the half of the greatness thereof was not told me. And when a soul by these gets in to our King Solomon, and is admitted to hear him by the gracious words of his mouth, speaking peace to a troubled soul, and comfort to a discouraged soul, answering all its doubts and hard questions; and withal admits the poor creature, lying under the deep sense of its own unworthiness, uncleanness, and undoneness, to a sight of his reconciled and lovely face, oh, how does this transport the creature to such an ecstasy of ravishment, as there remains no more spirit within her ! I bless Him for the many testimonies and evidences of his love to me and mine; for what I have gotten, and for what he has given me ground to expect ; for the performing of which I resolve to lie at his door all my days, for all my expectation is from him and in him ; and in his word do I hope, (Psal. cxxx. 5), for he has been better to me than ten sons.

- But after a little while word came, that some of the nobility of Scotland were turned popish, and that Popery was set up there. Upon which, misbelief and carnal reason told me that I needed not expect to see the performance of his promise upon which he had caused me to hope, which raised a new storm within me ; but faith (always a good friend in the time of trouble) brought that word in my mind, " How are they brought to ruin suddenly as in a moment ?" (Psal. lxxiii. 19).

One day, after I was under much doubting and fear, for His outward dispensations on the one hand, and a misbelieving heart on the other hand, were like to make me lose sight of the promises, I was much troubled, and knew not what to do. At last, I thought I would go to God, and seek help from him to resist the devil and an ill heart; and when I came into the room, I was in doubt whether to begin with reading or praying first; and when I thought how sweet he had made his word to me, it gave me ground to expect help from him in my straits. So I took the Bible, and that place was remarkably brought to me, "If ye abide in me, and my words abide in you, ye shall ask what ye will, and it shall be done unto you," (John xv. 7), which I thought was very remarkable, and bred new fears unto me. He let me see that there was something required on my part; my not abiding in him, and his words not abiding in me, might make him not to perform his promise to me. After I had read a little, I went to prayer, and while I was pouring out my spirit before him, he was graciously pleased to set home that word, "God is in the midst of her, she shall not be moved; God shall help her, and that right early," (Psal. xlvi. 5).

When I heard that the Parliament was to sit down, I was in great fear it should establish Popery, and make that Church which was once beautiful, base in the eyes of all nations. And I made it my errand to God, that he would not give them their will; and he brought those words to me, "Associate yourselves, and ye shall be broken in pieces; take counsel, and it shall come to nought; speak the word, and it shall not stand: for God is with us," (Isa. viii. 9, 10). Faith told me they should not get their will; misbelief said they should; and betwixt these two was I in great fears when the news came, (for they came every week), which made me again and again cry to Him, that he would remember his word on which he had caused me to hope; for I thought I had some grounds to believe that he would not leave that people. It was my suit to Him, that he would divide his enemies there, which he did, for he had told me, that a house divided cannot stand. And one time that word was set home to me, "Thy words are heard," wherein I cannot but admire his free love and gracious condescendency to such a piece of sinful clay as I am; for he divided them,

and let them not get their wills at that time. Now, who would
not serve so good a Master as he is,—who ever liveth to
make intercession for his people! I have good reason to
sing of the mercies of the Lord, and declare his faithfulness
to all generations.

But a little after, the cloud grew darker upon the Church;
and my ill heart and misbelief were like to make me give
over hopes that ever I should see good days. And one
time, while I was wrestling against misbelief and an ill
heart, He was graciously pleased to set home that promise,
" As one whom his mother comforteth, so will I comfort
you: and ye shall be comforted in Jerusalem. And when
ye see this, your hearts shall rejoice, and your bones shall
flourish like an herb: and the hand of the Lord shall be
known towards his servants, and his indignation towards his
enemies," (Isa. lxvi. 13, 14). I desire to bless him for it.
I can say, I have esteemed the words of his mouth more
than my necessary food, and that he never disappointed
me; and yet when I meet with a new difficulty, I have my
faith always a seeking, as to the making out of his promise
to me in particular, and to the Church in general; especially when his outward dispensations seem to contradict his
promises.

One day I received a letter from a friend, that my sons
did not mind their books as they should, which troubled me
much, and made me go to God for them many a time; for
I thought his outward dispensations seemed to contradict
his promise to me, for he inclined me early to give them to
him; ere ever they were born I gave them to him, and
afterwards in baptism, and often had covenanted them to
him and his service; and he had given me some grounds to
expect he had accepted the offer: but misbelief was like to
prevail too much with me. But one day I went to God,
and took with me his promise, " I will be your God, and the
God of yours," (Gen. xvii). And I pleaded the God of
that promise for me and mine, and took the place to witness
that I had offered them to him; and that I was content to

take him on his own terms, as he had offered himself in the
gospel; a King to rule over me and mine, and to defend
us from the evil of sin without; and a Saviour to save us
from the wrath of God; a Prophet to teach us, and his all-
sufficiency to provide for us. And while I was pouring out
my spirit before him in the behalf of me and mine, he was
graciously pleased to answer me with that promise, "Be it
unto thee as thou wilt," and through his grace I shall hold
by it all my days. And I charge all mine, as they shall
answer to God at the great day, and as they would not
have me to be a witness against them in that day, that ye
covenant yourselves away to God and his service, and plead
the good of this promise in particular, every one of you for
yourselves; for all I can do for you cannot merit heaven for
you: for with the heart man believes, and every man is
saved by his own faith. All my desire is, that He would
glorify himself, by redeeming me and mine from hell and
wrath, and make us useful in our generation for his glory.
I thought fit to write this for my own use and the good of
mine; and if the Lord should take me from them by death,
I hope the words of a dying mother shall have some impression upon their spirits.

A young man coming from Holland, brought me a letter
from my two sons, and told me he had brought two books
for me, viz. The Impartial Inquiry, and Essex Murder; but
having carelessly put them among his clothes, all were taken
together. I told him that I gave them no order to send me
such books, neither did my letter mention them. I advised him
also to go out of town, for they would seek after him; which
they did, by an order of the mayor of Newcastle (where I
then lived), within an hour after he went from my house.
It greatly troubled me, that any of mine should have been
the occasion of trouble, either to others or myself. I went
to God with it, having the experience that he was the hearer
of prayer, and presented his promise, which formerly he had
persuaded me of, that no plague should come near my
dwelling; that he should give his angels charge over

me ; that his faithfulness should be a shield and buckler to
me.   And when I was pleading with Him, that he would
rebuke the fury of the enemy, that they might not get liberty
to vent their malice against me, nor the young man, and
that none might be the worse for my sake, free love made
him to answer me with that promise, " He has delivered,
and he will deliver," (2 Cor. i. 10) ; and, " What I do thou
knowest not now, but thou shalt know hereafter," (John
xiii. 7), which gave me ground to believe that I, and those
concerned, should be delivered from that trouble.   But two
or three days after, the young man and his sister, and some
friends with them, came back to the town, to inform the
magistrates that those books were to me, thinking to free
themselves by laying the blame on me ; and when I heard
this, it put me to go more frequently to His door, and cry
for help : for many times faith is a seeking under new trials
and frowning providences, while as all ends in mercy to me.
I was impelled to plead with Him thus,—that if he would
perform the promise upon which he had caused me to rest
for deliverance out of this trouble, it should be a ground to
believe all the other promises he had given me for greater
things.   I cannot but admire His free love and care to me
and mine, for the net they spread for me they were taken
in themselves ; for the young man's sister was that night
laid in jail for keeping back her brother, and appearing herself, and the God of my fathers suffered them not to get
their designs towards me accomplished.   She was liberated
within a day upon bond to answer at the sessions.   It was my
desire to God, that he would put it in their hearts to give
them back their clothes and their books, which was fulfilled
half a year after ; only these pamphlets were, as some said,
sent to the king, or   *   *   *   *   *   *

March 5. 1687.   I went to God that day in behalf of me
and mine, and it was my desire to him that we might be
not only hearers, but doers of his will.   For when I heard
of the unsuitable practice of some, whose knowledge and
profession was great, it made me fear what I and mine might

do in dishonouring of him : and I poured out my spirit before Him who is the hearer of prayer, and was in good earnest with him, that I and mine might be among those that were on his heart that day that he spoke those words, "Father, I will that those whom thou hast given me be with me where I am ;" and that we might be early doers of his will, and some of them might be fitted for building his house, for I had given them to him. And while I was wrestling with him in prayer, free love made him to answer me in that promise, "Ask me of things to come concerning my sons, and concerning the work of my hands command ye me," (Isa. xlv. 11). It made me to wonder at free love, in his answering such a piece of clay as I am ; but free love has no reason, but because he WILL : and seeing he offered himself so freely to me, he helped me to be as free with him, in asking him, and taking from him ; for I took heaven and earth, and the place to witness that I would take him at his word. And my desires were, that I and mine might be doers of His will on earth, and for ever with himself in glory ; and he answered me with that promise, "Be it unto thee as thou wilt :" and through his grace I will keep that rich jewel all my days.

I thought then my mountain stood sure ; but ere ever I was aware, I met with a new trial, and I had my faith a seeking : for after a liberty to Popery was proclaimed in Scotland, I was like to lose sight of the promises. Carnal reason and misbelief had much to say : I made it my errand to him, that he would help me to get the mastery of these enemies ; and he was pleased to strengthen my faith in that promise, "After I have plucked them out, I will return, and have compassion on them," (Jer. xii. 15), which strengthened my faith, and my enemies within me were silent a little ; but soon after they got up upon me. His outward dispensations seemed strange-like ; for in England, where I lived, there was light of the gospel, and much liberty, but in Scotland much trouble, which was strange-like : and it was my desire to him to know what it spoke ; and he brought that word to my mind, "Rise and eat, for thou hast forty days to go in the strength of this meat;" upon which I feared there was a great storm coming upon England. I went to God, that he would remember his promise, that no plague should come near my dwelling, and that he should give his angels charge over me and mine ; and he promised me that his truth and faithfulness should be a hedge about me and mine ; and I placed them all there, and through his grace, they shall never be taken out again.

But when I began to think of the sad case of the Church of France, and other places beyond sea, how they had been sore troubled, and my native land, it made me to cry out, "Oh that my head were waters," &c., (Jer. ix. 1); yet I had reason to bless Him for the light of the gospel they had, though it was not a plenteous rain on such a weary heritage ; it made me to moderate the greatness of it, especially coming from a popish king. That place of Scripture, where Ahab proclaimed a fast, to get his wicked designs accomplished, was brought to my mind. It was my fear, that the enemies of the Church would stone the Protestant interest to death, under the pretence of giving a liberty ; the fear of this, made me to enjoy all my pleasant things with sorrow of heart. But the government is on His shoulders, and the poor of his people must trust in him. He abideth faithful, and cannot deny himself : that which he hath promised, he will perform.

One night, among many others, I could sleep but little ; but when I thought upon what he had promised to me and mine, and to the Church, and yet how his outward dispensations said the contrary, (for he had suffered the enemy to break the Church abroad and at home), I was presenting his promise to him, and telling him what fear and misbelief said, That I should not see his glory return to these covenanted lands, and mine should not be useful for building of his house. And while I was weeping and crying to him against my corruptions, which have never a good tale to tell of God and his dispensations, he set home that word to

my spirit, which refreshed me much, The Lord answered
the angel which talked with me, with good words and comfortable, that what he had promised, he would perform; he
would not suffer his faithfulness to fail; he was the God of
all flesh; there was nothing too hard for him; his house shall
be built again: and I answered, "Praise and glory be to
thee for ever and ever." I bless him that I can say I have
a Bethel, where I wept and made supplication to him, and
found him. His presence, his presence made up the loss of
my outward comforts to me; for my husband durst not stay
with me for near two years at that time. The circumstances
then made friends afraid to own me; but I bless Him, that
he thus made the nether springs to run dry upon me, for
that made me to seek the Fountain, where I was refreshed

The liberty for preaching was always the longer the
greater. The king sent out a proclamation, and promised
fair things.* I could not but wonder at it, he being a Pa-
pist; but that place of scripture was brought to my mind,
where Absalom stole away the hearts of the people by his
flattery, and while he pretended religion, there was mischief
in his heart. I wondered to see the people so taken with
it, which I was not. I went to God in these perplexities
of mind, and begged that the ministry of the word, which I
knew was to be performed by Dr Gilpin, (being his first
sermon in the meeting-house after liberty), might either
convince me or confirm me. When I went in at the door,
that word was borne in, "Eat thy meat with fear, and drink
thy water with trembling," (Ezek. xii. 18). When the
minister came in, he sung the 137th Psalm. His prayer
was all about the sad case of the church; his text, "O Lord,

* This was a "Declaration for liberty of Conscience," passed on
April 4. 1687, in which all the penal laws against Protestant Dissenters
as well as Papists, were suspended, all persons suffering prosecution on
account of violating them, were absolved; and full permission was given
to hold religious meetings, whether in houses or chapels, without molestation. The unthinking rejoiced in this toleration, which was in
fact merely designed for the relief of the Papists, and finally for the
re-establishment of Popery.

I have heard thy speech and was afraid: O Lord, revive thy work in the midst of the years, in the midst of the years make known; in wrath remember mercy," (Hab. iii. 2). And all his whole preaching confirmed me that sad days were yet coming. It was my errand to God, to know at that time his smiling on England so much, and frowning on Scotland (for there was no liberty granted then to it); and that place of Jonah's being sent to Nineveh, was cast in my mind, snewing me that He was sending his ministers to call England to repentance, or else he would take the scourge to them.

One night I was pouring out my spirit before God in behalf of my native land, that he would not make them a desolation; and I made use of this argument, that the great wickedness of those that were rulers, both in church and state, might move him to cast them out; and I got these words for an answer, "Thy words are heard," &c., which I hope in his own way and time he will make out.

It was still my fear that Popery would be set up, and it might come to my door, either to burn, or to deny Him; and then I considered how my corrupt nature, and the temptation meeting together, had made me to yield to little things. It was my desire to Him, that he would keep me through his power unto salvation; and he brought that place to me, "My grace shall be sufficient for thee;" and through his grace, I shall hold by it for me and mine all my days. One thing here is observable, that at the giving in of this promise, and all the rest, he helped me firmly to believe the accomplishment of them, as if I had seen it with my eyes; and yet between the passing and performing of some of those promises, many a sad and dark day I had. My misbelief made me often say, "Why art thou to me, O Lord, as waters that fail?" yet I can say, from good and frequent experiences, that they who sow in tears shall reap in joy.

The more I thought upon the case of the church for the present, and what we had formerly seen, and what ere long we were like to see, it made my sleep to depart from me; and one night being much taken up in thinking what might be the Lord's mind in the liberty that was granted, that scripture was given in, "Who shall entice Ahab to go up to Ramoth-Gilead? And there came out a spirit, and stood before the Lord, and said, I will entice him, by being a lying spirit in the mouth of all his prophets;" which seemed to presage, that his (James II.) following the counsel of his popish priests would tend to his ruin. And also, another sad thing was this unto me, to see the ministers that got the liberty, and the people, so silent against popery that they by those devices were bringing in. How sad was it to me, to see my Lord Christ wronged of his right, and of that gift which he got from his Father, viz. the utmost ends of the earth for a possession, and which by our fathers were so solemnly sworn away to him. If any were coming to take our possessions from us, how would we oppose them! But what little opposition was made against those that were risen up to wrong Christ of his right and possession! I fear that curse be due to many in these lands, which was denounced against Meroz, for not coming out to help the Lord against the mighty, (Judg. v. 23).

My husband got a call to Beverley, near an hundred miles south from Newcastle; then misbelief told me, that I needed not expect to see His glory return to Scotland, for carnal reason said I was turning my back on it; yet faith told me, it should be made out to me. One day I went to God for this, that he would make good his promise, on which he had made me to hope. He set home that word, " Blessed is she that believeth, for there shall be a performance of those things which were promised to thee by the Lord; and my presence shall go with thee." These promises were as refreshful to me as my daily bread. He helped me to submit to him, if my husband could be more useful in that place than another. But he could not be free to stay above four or five months with them, which gave me grounds to hope I should see my native land. After a while liberty for Scotland came out, but considering it came from a popish king, made me fear what the issue might be.

Afterward my sons came from Holland, and not meeting with that from them which I expected, bred new trouble to my mind ;—for I thought I had His promise that he would make them useful in the work of the ministry, having long ago dedicated them to that work, and having grounds to believe he had accepted of the offer, yet they were both against it, which gave my faith a sore set. Misbelief and an ill heart bade me cast away the child of promise ;—why should I wait any longer on the Lord? But love bade me hold by the promise. I went to God, and poured out my spirit in prayer. He opened mine eyes, and let me see a well in the wilderness, and faith brought me an olive leaf, viz. "If ye believe not, yet He abideth faithful, and cannot deny himself;" which was sweeter to me than the honeycomb.

The king was for taking away the penal statutes, and those of the Independent way in Newcastle were for it, which I thought sad, to hear the bairns of the house content to break down the hedge, and let in the wild beasts into the vineyard, which made me go to God, to know whether their way or Presbyterian government was the best. And these two scriptures, Acts 1st and 15th chapters, confirmed me in the latter.

I was regretting this to a good woman, their condescending too much to the king's devices for taking away the penal statutes; she told me, she heard that all the ministers of Scotland were for that too. I told her that I hoped God would never leave them so far. I came home to my house, and went to prayer, and poured out my spirit before Him, that he would remember his promise, on which in this matter he had caused me to hope, viz. That he would not forsake that land. I could sleep little that night, but cry and weep before him in behalf of the Church in that land: I told him, what a great dishonour to his name it would be, if he should forsake them, because he had owned them in such a singular manner to contend earnestly for the faith, and he had received a sacrifice of their hand, by their sealing of that truth with their blood: and he gave me his promise, that my words were heard; for he would see their ways and heal them; which eased my troubled spirit. But yet my faith was mixed with fear, which made me to go often to his door and knock; and I bless him he opened to me many a time, and refreshed me with the words of his mouth; but my corruptions and a body of death got too much the mastery of me, and laid me low.

One day I was speaking of the Church of Scotland to some; I told them that I hoped He would yet appear in his glory there, and that I should see it; and they told me, I might never see that, for Mr Livingston and Mr Wellwood, two famous ministers, had as great hopes to see that sight, and were disappointed; which took deep impression on my spirit, and I went to God and poured out my spirit before him, who I can say, is the Hearer of prayer, for I had experience, that in coming to him by prayer and reading the scriptures, I found a cure for all my distempers from him. I was like to lose sight of the promise; I told him, all these things were against me; misbelief, and an ill heart, and carnal reason, his outward dispensations, and the experience of his people, told me, that I might not expect that from him, that was but a woman, and so little a plant in his garden, when he had denied it to his faithful ministers; which brought me so low, that I was like to lose sight of the promises which he had given me, and helped me to believe that they should be made out to me, as if I had seen it with my eyes; and yet misbelief got the mastery of me. And while I was weeping and making supplication to him, faith brought me ease and quiet from that word, "He will perfect his praise out of the mouths of babes and sucklings; for he will hide that from the wise and prudent, and reveal it to babes and sucklings." And Manoah's wife saw more than the man; and Abraham's hoping against hope, that he was faithful who had promised, and was able to perform. Oh, how sweet these were to me! and set me on my feet again, and gave me new grounds of hope. I thought then, my mountain was sure, but ere I was aware, I was fast in the

miry clay of misbelief again; for a friend sent me a letter,
wherein he regrets the sad case of some of the godly
ministers in Scotland that had no liberty to preach.* And
when I thought of the liberty that was granted for all sorts of
errors, and a restraint on some of the godly ministers, and
none for my husband to preach there, all former experience
would not cure this fit of unbelief, till I made a new errand
to His door; and I bless him that ever I had so many errands, or else I had never known the freeness of the Giver,
and the goodness of the entertainment, if love and necessity
had not put me to be a beggar at his door. While I was
importunate with him by prayer, that he would remember
his promise on which he had caused me to hope concerning his
Church, he answered me, " I will work for my name's sake,
lest it should be polluted among the heathen;" and with that
promise, that the Church of Scotland should be called a
people redeemed of the Lord, sought out and not forsaken;
and that other promise, " Be it unto thee as thou wouldst."
These were more precious to me than thousands of gold
and silver. I can say (to his free grace be it spoken) I came
from him and my countenance was no more sad, for I had
light in the Lord. My petition was granted, that the rest of
the faithful ministers in that land should get their liberty;
and his glory should return to that land, and my eyes
should see it; which came exactly to pass, for which I desire

* In the first royal proclamation of Toleration for Scotland, which
was made February 12. 1687, only the moderate Presbyterians were
allowed to meet in private houses for religious exercises, but not to
build meeting-houses, or assemble in out-houses or barns. This permission was also coupled with an oath which the more conscientious
Presbyterians could not take. The Second Toleration, of March 31,
dispensed with the oath; and the Third, proclaimed June 28, allowed
as ample a liberty to Scotland as to England, with the exception of
right to hold field conventicles, which were still denounced. This last
permission, after some hesitation and discussion, was accepted in Scotland; in consequence of which Mr Veitch received a call from people
in the parishes of Oxnam, Crailing, Eckford, Linton, Morebattle, and
Hownam, to become their minister, and preach to them at Whitton-
hall, which lay adjacent to these several parishes.

to bless him for ever and ever, and through his grace shall go softly all my days.

The reading of Mr Andrew Gray on the Promises, and the Faith of Assurance and Prayer, Mr Rutherford's Letters, and Goodwin on Prayer, the Lord blessed them to me, for I was refreshed with them many a time; but his word was above all to me like Goliah's sword, there was none like it.

The reasons why I was so concerned for Scotland, were, 1st, That it was my native land. 2dly, It was most oppressed. And, 3dly, It had been in former times singularly owned of God; and I thought it would be a great dishonour for him to leave it. Yet I was not altogether confined to it; but He helped me to remember other places, and especially England, where I and my family had met with seventeen years' kind entertainment. When I went to God and poured out my spirit before him in behalf of England, he promised he would not make a full end, but wrath once would be upon them for their sins, if repentance prevent not. After we had been seventeen years banished from our native land, He performed his promise upon which he had caused me to hope; the king and council gave orders for our return anno 1688. The manner of performing His promise was wonderful. I never expected it should come from a popish king; but His ways are in the deep waters, and his footsteps past finding out. But this promise was no sooner performed, than Esau appeared before me, and Laban behind me. My sons, whom I had kept at the College at Utrecht, were both for being soldiers, which troubled my spirit much; for I thought I had some grounds to believe he would make them useful for building his house. I went to God, and poured out my spirit before him, who had heard me in the day of my strait many a time; but these Philistines that dwell within me, prevailed so much on me, and put out my eyes, that I could not see the wondrous things of his laws. He made me remember the miracle of the loaves which he had performed the other day, but all would not do. I was toiling in the duties of prayer, meditation, and reading of the word some days and nights, but caught little. All former experience would give me no ease to my troubled spirit, till I got new supplies.

One time I went and cast the net at his command, and there I was helped to bind them over to God, and if he had any service for them in that station of soldiers, I would submit. But I will be a beggar at his door all my days, and though he should slay me, I will trust in him: He answered me with that promise, "Thou shalt know that I am the Lord thy God, and none that wait on me shall be ashamed. And blessed be she that believeth, for there shall be a performance of these things which are promised to her of the Lord; and those that believe must not make haste: and trust in God when thou art in darkness, and hast no light, for he will perfect his praise out of the mouths of babes." Those promises gave some ease to my troubled spirit. I was in great strait what to do with them. I went to God and sought his counsel, because he had commanded me in all my ways to acknowledge him, and he would direct my steps. And when I was pouring out my spirit before Him, he brought these words into my mind, "Lay not thy hand upon the lad," for "he is a chosen vessel to me, to bear my name before the Gentiles;" and I answered, "Even so be it, O Lord." After I had tasted this honey that lies in the promises, mine eyes were opened a little; for which I desire to bless Him for ever and ever, that ever I had been refreshed with his promises, especially on the 1st of March and that 5th of January, the first week of April and the 20th day of April 1688. Let my soul never forget these times, and many other times when He and I met. I was not yet come out of England. I may say, it was like the river Chebar to me; then I saw the heavens opened, and the vision of God.

After I came into Scotland, it was upon my thoughts what God had done for me, what I had promised to him, and what he had promised to me. My promise to Him

was, that if he should bring me back to Scotland, I would set
some days apart, to bless Him for what he had done for
me and mine, and for his Church : and his promise to me
was eternal life to me and mine. The greatness of these
promises made me to fear that they should not be performed
unto me, because his word hath said, one of a tribe and
two of a family should be saved ; which put me to pour
out my spirit before Him in behalf of me and mine : but
he answered me with these words, " Though it be wonderful
in thy eyes, it is not so in mine, and my thoughts are not
as thine ;" which gave me ground to expect good from
Him ; yet my faith was mixed with fears. But one time,
when I was pleading the good of these promises, He inclined
my heart to ask a sign from him that my heart might be
more confirmed of the truth of it ; and the sign was, that
if He had accepted of me and mine, that they might evidence
by their practice, that they were bairns of the higher house,
and my eyes might see it. Free love made him to answer
me with these words, " Thy words are heard ;" for which
I bless Him, and through his grace shall be a beggar at
his door all my days, for the making out of these promises
to me and mine, and I charge all mine to do so.

His promise to me for his Church in Scotland was not
yet altogether performed. I was like Haman (Esther v. 13),
all availed me little, so long as I saw Popery and Prelacy
owned by authority. I thought that then the ark was
still in the house of Obed-Edom ; it was my desire He
would spirit some to bring it to Jerusalem. I was little more than half a year in Scotland till the Prince of
Orange came over to England, which made me to wonder
what could be the meaning of that dispensation ; for when
I was in England, He gave me grounds to believe, that
he would take the rod to that people, which made me to
have a holy fear of his threatenings, for he helped me to
believe, he was as just in performing his threatenings as
he is in his promises, if repentance do not prevent it ; and
yet, instead of taking the rod, he had raised up a Deliverer

for them.' I went to God to see what was his mind in this dispensation: He answered me, "What I do now, thou knowest not, but thou shalt know hereafter: a fire unblown shall consume them." Upon which I feared there was a stroke for England, which made me go to Him, that he would make repentance to prevent it. It was my desire to God, that he would make the Prince of Orange an instrument for the bringing down of Popery and Prelacy in Scotland, and that He would make good his promise to me which he promised in England, that they should be ruined in a moment. I cannot but wonder and admire at his free love and his faithfulness to me, in performing this promise; for when the Convention sat down, He spirited them to accomplish it.* I was still in a fear and some exercise of mind about the making out of His promises to me. Carnal reason and unbelief made me to charge Him foolishly, as if his death and sufferings could not reach me and all mine; which put me many a time to come to his door and cry for help, that I might be more confirmed of the truth of these promises, that he had redeemed me and mine. I cannot but admire his free love to me. When I was pouring out my spirit before him in prayer, he brought that word wonderfully to my mind, where the angel appeared to Cornelius (Acts x.), and bade him send for Peter, who would tell him words by which he and all his house should be saved. He opened mine eyes, and let me see that which I had never seen before so clearly; that Christ's death and blood could reach a whole family; for which I desire to praise him for ever and ever, that free love should have condescended to make use of such clay and spittle as me and mine, and to work a miracle of them. This gave me new ground to plead the promise for me and mine, and that the sign I sought from him might

---

* The Convention was held January 22, 1689, to call William to the vacant throne. Upon this occasion, Popery was voted to be inconsistent with the English Constitution, and all Papists were for ever declared incapable of succeeding to the crown.

be accomplished that they might evidence by their practice they were his, and my eyes might see it. And he promised me, my words were heard; and through his grace, I will be a beggar at his door all my days for the performing this promise upon which he hath caused me to hope; and I charge all mine to set some days apart, to plead the good of this promise for yourselves and the Church; and I promise in his name you shall be made welcome, and find good entertainment in his company: he will take you up to Mount Pisgah, and let you see a sight of the promised land, and the hope and assurance of it. It cannot be expressed what soul-contentment and consolation is to be had in setting some time apart, and leaving all things at the foot of the mount, and to go up by faith, and take a sight of the good land, and to get some of the fruits of it to feed on while you are here below. But, my dear bairns, come and see, and that will resolve the question best. I can commend it from the experience I have had, in setting some days apart to converse with God.

But still my wine is mixed with water: my two eldest sons came home from the college when the Prince of Orange landed in England, and they were both for being soldiers, which gave my faith a sore shock, because his outward dispensations seemed to contradict his promise to me; I thought it was laid in the grave, and misbelief made me sometimes say, " by this time it stinketh." Yet faith tells always good of God, that the needy should not always be forgotten, the expectation of the poor should not always perish. Love bade me remember the years of his right hand, and the wonders performed by the Lord to me, for I had some experience of the Physician, that he could make dead and dry bones live, and turn water into wine. This gave me ground to wait, if it were even to the eleventh hour; and though the vision tarry, wait for it, it would speak and not lie. Faith, love, and hope, told me, they should not die, but live and declare the works of God. Misbelief and a carnal heart, carnal reason and his out

c

ward dispensations their language said, they would both
be killed, for they were at the point of the sword. The
language of the two parties kept me at work, and put me
often to go to him to plead the good of the promises, that
he would give his angel's charge over me and mine, to
keep us in all his ways, and that his faithfulness might be
a shield and buckler to us to keep us in all our ways, and
to defend us from sin, and the wrath of cruel men. I had
this promise from him while I was in England, and when I
was in this strait, he helped me to plead the performance of
it; and faith told me, he would be as good as his word,
which I seek the making out of.

But still my faith was mixed with fears for the making
out of his promise to me and mine and his Church, and
though he had performed some part of his promise, in making
the Convention to condemn Prelacy, yet I thought Haman
high and Mordecai low when Presbytery was not settled;
I thought the ark was still in the house of Obed-Edom, and
that his promises, which he promised me in England, were
low and in the grave: and misbelief made me rove sometimes, and say, "Why art thou to me as a liar, or as waters
that fail?" I found it a great difficulty to believe in Him,
when his promise said one thing, and his providences said
another, though he had helped me to believe they would
be performed, as I had seen it with my eyes; and yet between the passing of the promise, and the performing of it,
I had many a sad and dark day. I may say, with great
wrestling did I obtain them, yet I cannot but commend the
riches of his free love; those that sow in tears, shall reap
in joy. If weeping be in the night, joy shall be in the
morning. Misbelief was often bidding me cast away the
child of promise,—why should I wait any longer on him?
But faith keeps always the dead grip: "Though thou
shouldst slay me, yet will I trust in thee." The grace of
patience told me, that they who believe, must not make
haste, "And thou shalt decree a thing, and it shall be done
unto thee."

These promises were as refreshing to me as my daily bread, yet I was still in fear about the ark. I was sometimes going about my watch, to see what would become of Scotland's Moses that was hid among the bulrushes; the glorious work of Reformation, who would draw it out? If I might speak it with reverence, I thought God was become my debtor by promise for Scotland, and for mine, and I would seek the performance of both these promises. He promised me, they should be called a people redeemed of the Lord, sought out and not forsaken. And when Melvil was made Commissioner, I went to God when the Parliament was to sit down, and begged of him, that he would stir up the king and rulers of the land, that God would spirit them to own a broken covenant and work of reformation, and purging of his house, and casting out those who had run and God had not sent them, and bring home the ark to Jerusalem, and building the hedge of discipline about it; and that his glorious presence might be seen in owning the doctrine and discipline of his own house by Presbytery, that all who hear and see it, shall be forced to acknowledge that it is God's way.

One day I was reading the Acts of the General Assembly, where I found, that God had honoured Scotland in making them zealous for his glorious interest, in owning them in this land; and had made them helpful to England, Ireland, and other places beyond sea. I went to God with these words which Moses made use of for the Church of the Jews, when the Lord seemed to be angry with them, that he would "remember his covenant with Abraham, Isaac, and Israel:" I thought Scotland had a good right to these promises, and I begged for Christ's sake, that he would remember our Abrahams, Isaacs, and Israels that had entered into a covenant with him, and had contended for the faith delivered unto them, and some of them had sealed it with their blood. And while I was pouring out my prayer before him, free love made him to answer me with these words, " The glory of the latter house shall be greater than the glory of the former," for which I desire to praise him for ever and ever.

But I was in a new trouble, for word came that there was a whole regiment of foot and a troop of dragoons cut off in the Forth, and fear, carnal reason, and misbelief, bade me cast away the child of promise, for my sons were now gone. I went to God in prayer, and it was my desire to uncover the roof of the house, and let down the promises on which he had caused me to hope for his church in general, and mine in particular, which I thought were lame. He helped me to believe he could make them both to walk; and when I was pleading with him in prayer, he set home that word, "Though thou walk in the midst of troubles I will revive thy spirit; I will stretch forth mine hand against the wrath of thy enemies, and his right hand shall save thee. He will perfect what concerns thee, for his mercy endures for ever. He will not destroy the works of his own hands." This promise was as refreshing to me as my daily bread.

This promise was also made out to me, for no evil befell them at that time. I can say from experience, that he is the hearer of prayer; and they that sow in tears shall reap in joy.

When I heard of the sad case that Mr Riddel was into in France, and when I thought how God had heard me in many particulars, it gave me encouragement to go to God on his account. It was my desire to God that he might be preserved and brought back again to his native land, and made useful in his vineyard: and while I was pleading with God in prayer on his behalf, he answered me with these words, "After I am sanctified in him in the sight of the heathen, he shall return; he shall not die, but live, and declare the works of God;" upon which he helped me through faith to grip these promises, that they should be accomplished.

This promise seemed Lazarus-like, to be laid in the grave a long time, which put me to go to God for him many a time, and beg for Christ's sake, that he would remember his word upon which he had caused me to hope. He performed this promise to me, and brought him back again to Scotland, where he preacheth the gospel.* I may say he was an Isaac to me, the child of promise, and a Samuel both, the son of prayer; for a year and a half together, there was not a day past over my head, but I was at God's door crying to him on his behalf, though I can say from good experience, he can make dead and dry bones to live.

After my husband had been two years preaching in a meeting-house in Teviotdale, the government being settled, he got several calls to kirks; but they being lame in some things, he could not embrace them, which was like to occasion many to speak of him, which was a trouble to my spirit. I went to God, to know his mind, which of the cities of Judah he would have me to dwell in : I desired to be where me and mine could be most useful for God : I knew he ceased to speak to me as he did to David, but it was my desire to him, that he might make it appear in his providence remarkable to me, that I might know his mind where to dwell. I cannot but observe how wonderfully he answered me. A friend of mine living thirty miles off the place where I lived, wrote my husband a letter desiring him to come and see her, for she was in a very sad case. He was unwilling to go, but I urged him sore to go; upon which he took horse, and riding all night, when he came near Peebles, being wearied, he asked a herdman on the way, Who kept an inn at Peebles? He directed him to Provost Muir's, and when he came and sat down, and had refreshed himself a little, he and some other strangers began to discourse about Teviotdale. The Provost hearing, asked if he knew one Mr William Veitch that lived there? He said he knew him.

---

* Mr Archibald Riddell was minister of Kippen. He was imprisoned in the Bass, but liberated in 1685, on condition of his transporting himself to America. On his return home in 1689, the ship in which he sailed was captured by a French vessel, and himself thrown into prison in France, where he endured great hardships. He was released through the interposition of King William, and after his return to Scotland he became minister of Kirkcaldy.

He speired if he was at home? and he said No, he was not
at home. My husband asked at him what he would do
with him? He told him, they had a mind to call him for
their minister, and they had hired a man, and written a
letter, and the man was going to his house with it, to desire him to come and preach to them on the Sabbath-day.
My husband told them that they needed not to trouble
themselves, for they would not get him at home, nor yet to
be their minister, as he thought, for he had several calls in
his own country. The Provost not knowing him all this
time, but after some more discourse, he asked at my husband if he was the man they were seeking? He told them
he was the man, which made them both to wonder at that
piece of providence. He took horse, and rode ten miles
further west, to see my friend; but they engaged him to
come back that way to preach to them, which he did. After
he came home, he told me. I was put to wonder; I was,
like Abraham's kinsmen, made to say, "It is of the Lord;
I can neither say good nor bad." They drew up a call to
him, and sent to the synod, where they condescended unto
it, and my husband embraced it; but yet out of this
pleasant rose there sprang many a thorn, for both friends
and foes were ready to reproach him, which was a trouble
to my spirit, to see the people one day idolize him, and
another day reproach him, because he would not stay
with them. I went to God with these words that David
went with, "Help, Lord, for I am become a reproach
unto them; let them curse, but bless thou, and let them
know it is thy hand, and thou hast done it."

It was my desire to God that he would shew the gospel
a token for good to Peebles, that they that hated it might
see it and be ashamed; but the cloud grew thicker and
darker, for Queensberry and his Chamberlain were great
enemies. They came all that length, as to print a number
of lies against the presbytery and my husband, because
they could not get in one Mr Knox, who was a curate, and
cousin-german to John Balfour's lady. When I began to

consider that it was the glory of God, and the good of the Church, which they were like to break, and when John Balfour, and some others with him, went in to the General Assembly to petition them for Mr Knox the curate, I set a day apart and spent it in prayer in behalf of his Church, and he was pleased to answer me with that promise, " They shall fight against thee, but not prevail, for I am with thee, saith the Lord : what wicked men do most desire, shall utterly decay ; and mischief shall hunt the violent man, till he be ruined." Upon which he helped me to believe that these promises should be accomplished ; yet, when I heard that Queensberry had too many to own him in that affair, carnal reason was often saying as Gideon did, " If the Lord be with us, how can all this evil befall us ?" But faith let me see, that whom He loveth he chastens ; and he can let an Esau appear before, and a Laban behind.

I made it my errand to God, that he would not suffer Queensberry and all that took his part to break the gospel in Tweeddale. He answered me with that promise, "They shall return with shame to their own land ;" and that, "No weapon formed against Zion shall prosper ; every tongue that rises in judgment, thou shalt condemn : this is the heritage of the servants of God." I thought these promises were too great for such a piece of sinful clay as I am ; but love and necessity made me to take hold on them, and He was graciously pleased to make them out to me, for all they could do could not get in the curate : so that I can say from experience, that all the power and wit that the enemies have, cannot mar or break the promises of God. And yet, when I meet with new difficulties, I have often my faith a seeking ; and beggars get upon horseback, while princes walk upon foot. But this is my mercy, that He is a God that changes not, and therefore I am not consumed.

I bless the Lord, who kept me from being of a revengeful spirit. Whatever I met with from the creature, He helped me always to look to God. That was often upon my spirit which David said, "Let him alone ; God hath

bidden him ;" and that word in the Psalms, " Fret not thyself because of evil-doers." I was speaking with a minister,
who told me what a great enemy to the Church Queensberry was ; and when I thought how God had heard me in
many particulars, it was my desire to God that he would
not suffer him always to be an enemy to the Church. He
answered me with that promise, " I will pull him down out of
his dwelling-place, and root him out of the land of the living." He helped me to believe that he should not be long
an enemy to the work of God ; yet, a little after, I heard
he was going to London, and some other Lords with him,
to petition the king to get in the curates again. I was in
great fear about the work of God, and went to God with
that prayer which David did, " Grant not, O Lord, the desire of the wicked ;" and he answered me with that,—
" Fear them not, for the eyes that have seen them shall see
them no more, for the Lord fighteth for you." This gave
me grounds to believe that it should be well yet with the
Church.

But within a little after, the king wrote down a letter to
the Assembly, to put in a number of curates ; and because
they would not grant his desire, he dissolved them. This
put me again to go to God in behalf of his Church. It was
my fears that they would mar a begun work of reformation ;
but that promise in Isaiah vii. 5, 6, 7, was set home on my
spirit, " They have taken evil counsel against Judah, saying,
Let us go up and vex it ; but thus saith the Lord God, It
shall not stand, neither shall it come to pass." This promise was sweet and savoury unto me ; he helped me to believe that all the malice of wicked men should not get their
designs accomplished against the work of God. But a little
after, Queensberry, with some others with him, who had
been great enemies to the work of God, was put in public
place ; which put me to go to God's door again, that he
would remember his word to me, upon which he had caused
me to hope, for I thought his outward dispensations seemed
to contradict his promise. My spiritual enemies were like

to bring up an ill report of Him, and of his ways; and when I was pouring out my spirit before him, He set home that promise to me which Caleb and Joshua said to the children of Israel, "Fear them not, their strength is departed from them, and the Lord is with us," (Numb. xiv. 9). Oh, how refreshing was that promise to me! He let me see, in some part, as Elisha's servant, "There are more with us than against us," (2 Kings vi. 16). And yet, when I meet with new troubles, I have often my faith a seeking.

When I heard that Cannon, Buchan, and the French were coming into Scotland, I was in new fears again that they would swallow up the Church, that was, as it were, newly brought out of Egypt. All former experience could do but little in helping me, till I got new supplies. I went to God, and begged for Christ's sake that he would break their purposes against the work of God; and he set home that promise to me which he promised Hezekiah, "The prayer which thou hast prayed against Sennacherib, I have heard," (2 Kings xix. 20). I desire to bless Him who performed it, for he brake them.

When I began to consider the Lord's dealing with me and mine, in casting our lot to be in Peebles, where I had met with trouble; and though the presbytery had placed my husband according to the act of Parliament, that his enemies could find no blame in it, he had the call of the elders, heritors, and town-council, and the generality of all the people, and he referred his cause to the General Assembly; and though two Assemblies sat, yet not one of them determined about him. This put me to go to God, to see what his mind was in it, for those who should have befriended him did not own him. Then that word in Daniel x. 13 was brought to my mind, "The prince of Persia withstood me one and twenty days." I got faith's eyes from him, to see that the promise which He promised me, when I came first to Peebles, behoved to be accomplished,—"They shall fight against thee, but not prevail." "The vision is for an appointed time; though it tarry, wait for it; it will speak, and not lie."

These promises gave me ground to believe, that the enemies of the gospel in Peebles were permitted to fight so long against the gospel, and no longer than he pleased; but the great Angel of the Covenant should make good his promise: What they do most desire shall utterly decay, and much of his power and love should be seen in owning his gospel in Peebles; and much of his friends' weakness did appear, who should have owned it, and durst not for fear of man. But I may say, Happy is the man who hath the God of Jacob for his refuge; He will not disappoint them. I can say from frequent experience, it is better to put trust in the Lord, than to put confidence in riches or in princes.

But I was in a new strait again when the king ordered Angus's regiment to go to Flanders, my eldest son being a lieutenant there. Carnal reason and misbelief said, I could never see the promise accomplished. I went to God and pleaded with him that he might not fall into the hands of the enemy, and he promised me that he should not die, but live, and declare the works of God. He helped me to believe that his promise should be made out to me; and yet, when the news came that the colonel, lieutenant-colonel, and major were killed, carnal reason and fear, and his outward dispensations, were like to make me call in question the truth of the promise. I was often charging my soul to be silent before him; and when I was in the midst of this strait, faith brought this promise to my mind, "Hath he not spoken, and will he not also do it?" He helped me to believe that he should not die, but be either wounded or taken, which was wonderfully made out to me; for the day after the fight he wrote a letter to his father, that he was shot through the left cheek, an inch below the eye; the bullet falling into his mouth, he spat it out, and the marks of the blood were upon the letter he wrote, which came from his wound. When the news of it came to me, I was put to admire his free love and faithfulness to such a worm as I am. I can say from good experience, that he hath made good that promise to me, "Ask and it shall be given, knock and it shall be opened."

When I lived in England, in the parish of Langhorsly, in Stanton, there was a remarkable providence fell out. One Mr Thomas Bell, who was a Scotsman, and born in the parish of Westruther, my husband's brother being minister there, took care to get him educated, and afterwards coming to England, was Curate in Langhorsly. He was a great enemy to my husband, because some of his hearers withdrew from him, and would not hear him; upon which he informed the justices of peace all that he could against my husband, which put the justices to come and search for him: but they got him not at that time. He was often heard say, that he would either ruin my husband, or he him. When Major Oglethorpe* came to Morpeth, to lie with his dragoons, it pleased God to let my husband fall into his hands, and a party with him, who took him on the 19th day of January, about three or four o'clock in the morning, to Morpeth, till the king sent down an order to remove him to Scotland, three or four days after he was taken.

One William Colinwood, who lived in Mr Bell's parish, came to see me. He had been once a hearer of his, but had withdrawn, and heard my husband. He was going to Mr Bell to pay him some tithes; I desired him to come back by me, and tell me what Mr Bell said of my husband: for I said, 'tis like now he may think he has got his desire accomplished. William told me, he bade him go to Edinburgh and get a preaching, for he would be hanged against Tuesday. He said, How thought he to escape the just judgment of God, such a rebel as he? When he told me, that Scripture was on my mind, "Let them curse, but bless thou;"

---

* Major Oglethorpe, afterwards Sir Theophilus Oglethorpe, visited Mr Veitch many years after, when he was comfortably and honourably settled at Dumfries. Matters, however, had gone very differently with the knight, who was now poor and neglected; and he complained to the minister, that he had not only lost the reward for his (Mr Veitch's) apprehension, and other such services, but all his property besides. Veitch not only forgave him all past injuries, but made him a handsome present.

and that also, " He that rendereth evil for good, evil shall not depart from his house," (Prov. xvii. 13).   He was just going to Newcastle when he spoke to William Colinwood; he stayed all night, and came the next day to Pontisland, where he drank till ten o'clock at night with the Curate. There was a great storm of snow on the ground, and that day there had been a thaw.   He would be home that night. They took his watch from him, and his horse they locked up in the stable, but all would not do; he told them there was no fear, for he had a good horse.   So they gave him his horse, and nobody knew what way he rode; but he was found twelve nights and a day afterwards, standing in a water, frozen just to his arm-pits, dead, (for there came on a great frost again that night).   His hat was on, his band dry, his gloves on : he standing at the side of the water, had worn his boots and gloves to get out of the water.   They could scarcely get as many countrymen as to carry him home; and getting fore-hammers, they brake the ice, and tied him on a horse, and carried him to his wife.   The whole country about was astonished at that dispensation, and often said to me, there would none trouble my husband again ;—for they all knew that he was an enemy to my husband.   I told them, they that would not take warning from the word of God, would never take warning from that.   That Scripture was often borne in upon my spirit, " Rejoice not at the fall of thine enemy, lest He see it and be displeased;" and though He made out that promise to me, " Evil shall hunt the violent man, till he be ruined;" for we never wronged him, but much good had he gotten from my husband's bro-ther.   But I bless the Lord, I was not in the least lifted up with it; for his word was my counsellor: in all my doubts and fears it was as refreshing to me, as ever meat and drink were.   There are none that study to make the word of God the rule of their walk, and when grace is master of the house, but they will say, as David said when Shimei railed on him, " Let him alone, God hath bidden him, who knows but he will requite blessings for cursings?" But when corrupt nature is master, it will say, "Cut off the head of the dog;" but I am much in grace's debt, that kept me back from being of a Shimei's frame. But I could not but read much of God in it; for the net which the enemy spread for my husband, they were catched in it themselves: for my husband lived many years after that time, so that I may say, He hath made good that promise to me,

> "What wicked men do most desire,
> Shall utterly decay."

When the magistrates of Edinburgh were turned out, I was in new fears about the Church. I thought it was the design of Sanballats and Tobiahs, to bring our brother Esau, the bishops and curates, into the vineyard of the Lord, who had casten off all pity, whose anger had burnt perpetually, and had pursued their brother with the sword. It was my desire to God, that he would break their designs; and when I began to consider how God had raised up my Lord Warristoun his son, and had made him Secretary to King William, I thought he was Mordecai-like come to court. And I made it my errand to God in his behalf, that he would spirit him to bring down the proud Hamans; for I knew, that at such a time as that, he was brought to the kingdom: and He answered me with these words, "According to thy desire, so be it unto thee." But before I got this promise, it cost me many a prayer, both in the night and in the day. This gave me ground to believe, that it should be well with the Church; yet when I heard some news, that the king would still be a friend to the curates, I thought it strange-like,—it seemed to contradict His promise to me. But that word was wonderfully brought to my mind, "They are but (Haman-like) invited to dine with the king and queen." And when the Parliament was to sit down, it was my desire to God, that he might spirit them to own the work of God; and he promised me, He should "make the earth to help the woman," which promise he wonderfully made out.

When my youngest daughter was a-dying, it was my desire to God, that he would make good his promise to me, which he had promised me ten years ago, that she might give evident token of her being in Christ before he removed her off this world. And I thought his outward dispensations seemed to contradict his promise there; for she desired not to hear of death spoken to her. I went to God to see what his mind was in that dispensation. He bade me trust in him at all times, for I knew not what a day might bring forth. Oh, sweet was this promise to me as ever my meat and drink was; for He helped me to believe there should be a remarkable change on her, which he was graciously pleased to make out; for before she died, her father having been at prayer, she cried out, " Now I am content to leave you all," and inquired at me, whether or not we should know one another in heaven? I told her, I thought so. I questioned her, if she thought she should win there? She said, she hoped so. I asked if she prayed any? She said, she had prayed as long as she dought; she told Christ, that she was but a poor blind thing, and that she knew not the way, and that she. begged for Christ's sake, that he would lead her in the right way, and have mercy on her soul. She died with as much composedness, as if she had been going to see a friend, and without any pain; but kissed her father, mother, and sisters, and bade us all farewell. So He gave me good ground to believe that she is asleep in Christ. I have many experiences, that they that sow in tears shall reap in joy; for there were few days of ten years that ever passed over my head, but she was upon my spirit for the making out of this promise; and when it was made out, it was sweeter to me than thousands of gold and silver.

But I was in new fear again, about the making out of His promise; for word came, that King William and the king of France were going to fight, and my two oldest sons being in the camp with them, fear and misbelief were like to make me, Hagar-like, to cast away the child of promise, I went to God with that, " All things, whatsoever ye shall ask in prayer, believing, ye shall receive," (Matt. xxi. 22), and my desire to God was, that they should be preserved from the wrath of cruel men; for I had his promise long before, that no evil should befall them. Yet when I heard there were so many killed, I was in great fears about making out of the promises. And one day I went to God with that desire, Thou wilt fulfil thy promise to them that fear thee; thou wilt hear and save them. And while I was weeping and crying to Him, he set home that promise to me, "A thousand shall fall at their side, yet shall it not once come nigh them." I thought it was a great promise for such a worm as I was, but necessity and love made me to take hold of it; yet before it was accomplished, it cost me many a tear and prayer, for five weeks' time I could never hear from them. Sense, reason, and misbelief their language was, that they were killed. But faith, love, and hope, they told me, He had delivered, and would deliver them, and those that wait upon him, should not be ashamed; He has delivered them in six troubles, and in seven there shall no evil befall them. Wherever faith grips at the promise, sense and misbelief say, Shoot neither at great nor small, but faith, which is like the king of Israel. But faith's language is, "Though he slay me, yet will I trust in him."

I went to God to see what was his mind in it, that I could hear no particular word from them: He answered me with these words, "Though the vision tarry, yet it will speak and not lie." This promise was as refreshing to me, as my daily bread; and that,—"The prayer of the destitute he will surely regard, by him it shall be heard." And near five weeks after, He made good his promise; for they sent a letter, telling that they were both alive. When the letter came to my hand, I was put to say, as Hezekiah, "What shall I render unto thee, O thou preserver of men?" I have many a stone that I have taken out of Jordan, which I have set up in remembrance of God's goodness to me, mine, and his Church; but I may say, such mercies as these are not got but by fasting and prayer.

But again I was in a new fear, for when I heard that my eldest son was upon the sea, coming from Flanders to Scotland, the storm was so violent, that scarce was ever the like of it known; and when I understood they had been upon the sea many days, and no word came from them, sense, reason, and misbelief said he was gone; and His outward dispensations said so too, for the public news gave an account that all that were in the ship were cast away.

In this great strait, I went to God by prayer, and He helped me to believe that there was help laid upon one who is mighty to save; but fear and reason said, it was impossible he could be saved. And while I was pouring out my spirit before God in prayer, faith brought me that promise, "He hath delivered and he will deliver;" and that, likewise, "One like the Son of God walking in the midst of the fire," can keep him from being consumed. After I had tasted of the honey that lieth in this promise, I was comforted, believing that he would not die at that time. This promise was wonderfully made out, for after they had been for fifteen or sixteen days tossed up and down the seas, he was necessitated to leave that ship by reason of the scarcity of provision; and within a few days after he came out of it, it was cast away, and all that were in it were drowned. He was tossed again in that other ship fifteen days longer; and when he saw that there was no hope of escape, they were forced to run the ship as near the shore as they could, and after all to leap into the sea; and the violence of the waves broke the fore-part of the ship before he leaped out. The country people made them all the help they could, and so brought them half dead to land.

When he came home and told me this, I was put to wonder and admire, and cry out, "O thou preserver of men! what shall I do unto thee, who hast brought the promise through the grave, and performed it unto me?" I have good reason to say, that they who wait on thee shall not be ashamed.

My second son was still in Holland. He wrote that he

was fallen sick, and that the doctor said he was in a consumption. Fear and misbelief said he would die: it was my desire to God that he might be spared. He answered me with that promise, " I change not, and therefore he shall not be consumed, and his life shall be a prey to him in all places; and when he passes through the waters, I will be with him." This was remarkably made out, for after he came home, he told me that they were twice at sea, and by the violence of the storm were beaten back again; and there was a ship cast away just beside them, with a number of passengers. But I have experience that God's promises can neither die nor drown; and can say from the same good experience, that I had more soul-pleasure and contentment in the praying for, than ever I had in the enjoyment of those promises.

After I had been near four years in Peebles, my husband got a call to Paisley, another to Dumfries, and another to Edinburgh, but he would embrace none of them; wherefore they appealed to the General Assembly, and when it sat down, he desired them to vote whether he was legally settled in Peebles or not, because Queensberry and others alleged the Presbytery had not legally settled him there; and they did so, voting him all legally settled in Peebles. Then they called him, to see if he was content to leave Peebles. He told them with tears, that seeing he had God's call to that place, he would be content to stay in it; and his discourse which he then had, made some of them to weep. However, they put him out, and then voted, Transport or not transport. And Peebles (within five votes) carried it, although there were three parties against it. Next again, they voted which of the three should carry it, which Dumfries did; all which time they never so much as asked him what call he would most willingly embrace. When the news came to my ears, I was put to wonder. I went to God, to see what His mind was in removing the gospel from Peebles, and that word was set home on my spirit, " I must needs go through Samaria;" which gave me ground to be-

D

lieve the gospel had somewhat ado in another place. But my husband would not embrace the call, giving several reasons wherefore he could not.

When I began to consider on the sad case of Peebles, sense and reason, those two bold creatures, were like to quarrel with God, why such enemies of the Church as Queensberry should get so much of their will as to lay Peebles desolate; and that scripture was remarkably set home to me, "If thou seest the oppression of the poor, and violent perverting of justice and judgment in a province, marvel not at the matter, for He that is higher than the highest regardeth, and there be higher than they." And that scripture, "He that was before was afraid of his day, and he that cometh after shall be astonished." This gave a stroke to my spiritual enemies within; but they soon got up on me again, for my husband would not at all condescend to go to Dumfries.

This dispensation put me often to go to God, and to inquire, with Rebecca, Why am I thus? For he seemed to be angry; and that was the thing I most desired, that mine might be useful in his vineyard, and he seemed by his outward dispensations to say the contrary, especially when I had waded through my Jordan, and come to the good land. And one while, when I could sleep none, I was desiring to know His mind in it, he answered me with these words, "If the world hate you, it hated me before; be of good cheer, I have chosen you out of the world." It is better felt than can be told what joy and pleasure I met with in that promise,—more than all the trouble I met with before.

All this time my husband would not hear of going to Dumfries, and my spiritual enemies, misbelief and an ill heart, made me to quarrel with God; for when I came first to Peebles, I had this promise, that the enemies should fight against me, but not prevail. Sense and reason began to interpret his dispensations wrong, saying, "Why art thou to me as a liar, and as waters that fail?" for Queensberry and his party had got much of their will. It was

therefore my desire to God, that he would give me grace
and strength to get the mastery over my spiritual enemies,
that I might not charge him foolishly; and at length faith
and love, who have never an ill tale to tell of God, but are
good interpreters of his dispensations, their language was,
That he had made out that promise to thee, as well as to
Jeremiah; for the Lord permitted his enemies to put him
both in the dungeon and stocks, and yet the enemy had not
got power over thy husband, though they would as fain
have done it; and that which they most desired had de-
cayed, which was to get in curate Knox the first half-year
that he came to Peebles; and all their wit and malice
could not get it done, for your husband was permitted of
God to preach there four years, so that it was well made
out, what they most desired did utterly decay, for they
never thought he should have preached half a year there.

As yet, my husband would not condescend to go to Dumfries. It was my desire to God, He would incline his heart
to embrace that call where he might be most useful to God;
and at length the Commission of the Kirk prevailed with
him to go to Dumfries, about a quarter of a year after he
had been appointed by the Assembly, and that very day
four years after I came to Peebles, that very same day I came
out of it for Dumfries; and I would not have wanted the
experience of God's goodness and free love to me, mine,
and the Church, for all the trouble I met with in it. I can
say from good experience, it was like Mizar and Hermon
Hill to me.

After I came to Dumfries, I presented two petitions to
God: one was, that he would give success to the gospel;
the other was, that he would remove the division that was
in that corner. And that scripture was set home on my
spirit, "Their right eye shall dry up, and their right hand
shall wither," (Zech. xi. 17). When I had been about
two months in Dumfries, there came one from Peebles to
see me, who told me that Queensberry was still a great
enemy to Peebles Sense and reason again began to quar-

rel with God, that he was not so good as his promise, for
when I was in Peebles, He promised me that he would pull
him out of the land of the living, and the eye which had
seen him should see him no more; and yet there was no
appearance of performing this promise. It was therefore
my desire to God, that He would remember his words unto
me, upon which he had caused me to hope. But faith told
me, that they which believe should not make haste; and
indeed I was scarce half a year in Dumfries, till death
pulled him out of the land of the living, and that promise
was made out, "The eyes which have seen him shall see
him no more," for he never went after that to London to
see the king any more. I have therefore reason to walk
humbly in the bitterness of my soul all my days, for He
hath both said it, and himself hath done it. I have likewise reason to sing of the mercies of the Lord, and declare
his faithfulness all day long.

When the ships went away from hence to America, my
second son went as captain with them. I went to God in
prayer on his behalf, and the behalf of them who went with
him. My desire was, that they might be preserved, and
might be instrumental in setting up a gospel-church there,
and that it might be to turn away some from serving idols,
to serve the living God; yet I had my own fears that mine
might never win that length. And that scripture in Jeremiah xxiii. 23, was brought to my mind, "Am not I a God
afar off, as well as near-hand?" Which quieted my mind
much; and the Lord was pleased to make it good to me,
for the first letter ever we got from him, he told us he had
never been sick the whole way.

But soon after, I was put in new fear again; for he wrote
a letter, that they were fallen in blood with the Spaniards,
and they were like to be in strait for want of help from
Scotland, and that ere it were long, it was like it would
either prove a grave or a fortune. It was like Esau's four
hundred men coming against Jacob. It feared me much to
hear of this, and I went to God in this strait, who had

heard me often in a day of trouble; and it was my desire to God, that he would not let them fall into the hands of cruel enemies, as the Spaniards: and that scripture was put in my mind, " He hath delivered from the paw of the lion and bear, and he will deliver also from the hand of these uncircumcised Philistines ;" which eased my mind. But within a little, misbelief and an ill heart raised a new storm within me, that he was killed ; but I had former experience, that the best way to calm this storm, was by setting a day apart for prayer alone, and reading of his word. I went to God on his behalf, and poured out my spirit before him, that he would remember his word to me, upon which He had caused me hope. And while I was in prayer, that scripture was remarkably set home upon my spirit, " He shalt not die, but live, and shew the salvation of God." It was as refreshing to me, as ever my meat and drink was. And I cannot but observe God's goodness to me, in performing his promise to me in some measure ; for that very day I got a letter from Caledonia. Yet I was still in fear of them; because the Spaniards, French, Dutch, and English were against them.* I went again to God by prayer, that he would not let them fall into the hands of their adversaries, and that scripture was borne in upon me, which Hezekiah said to the people, " The arm of flesh is with them, but the Lord our God is with us, to fight for us, and to help us," (2 Chron. xxxii. 8). But I still was in a fear of them ; for I thought Moab, and Ammon, and Amalek, with Lot's children, were conspired against them. It was my desire, that God would not give them their will ; for I thought the devil with all his instruments had conspired to hinder the setting up of a gospel Church there. And my request to God was, that He would purge out these that were ill among themselves ; for I thought a mixed multitude had gone there. I went often to God, with that petition in my mouth, which David hath, " Lord, grant them not their desires, further

* This was the splendid scheme of colonizing the Isthmus of Darien, which was ruined by the jealousy of the above-mentioned nations.

not their wicked devices;" and that scripture was borne
home upon my spirit in prayer, "They have taken evil
counsel against Judah to vex her, but it shall not stand,
neither shall it come to pass."

When I received another letter from my son, he seems
not to be pleased, that they send not over help to them;
and when I hear the ill carriage of some of themselves, it
put me in a new fear again about them. And when I began
to consider, that though there was a mixed multitude
amongst them, yet they were in covenant with God; and
when I observed how God had remembered his covenant
with Abraham, Isaac, and Jacob, long since, it was my suit
to God, that he would hear the prayers of his people on
their behalf, and that the words of that Psalm might be accomplished, "The prayer of the destitute he will surely regard, by him it shall be heard." When I was pouring out
my spirit to Him on another account, this was brought to
my remembrance, which I hope in due time he will make
out.

Now, when the next fleet were to go, wherein Mr Sheills
and the rest were to go, my eldest son went a counsellor
with them. It was my desire to God, that they might be
preserved in health and strength, and win safely there to
help their brethren; for I thought they were like Judah,
both Ephraim and Manasseh were joined against them to
vex them: and that that promise in Isaiah to the Jews,
might be made out to them, "It shall not come to pass,
neither shall it be:" and that the ministers going might
come there with the fulness of the blessings of the gospel of
peace. But when I looked for good, behold evil came; for
it pleased the Lord to let the enemy break their design of
planting a gospel church in that place in the world.

This was like to raise a great storm; misbelief and carnal reason were like to charge Him foolishly, why he suffered his enemies to break so glorious a design, and gave
his people the wine of astonishment to drink; for the
Spaniards came with eleven ships against them, and England

was a great enemy to them, and they were necessitated to leave that place of the world. All these things were against me, and raised an exercise of spirit in me. I was, like the disciples, in a mistake; I thought He would have restored the kingdom to Israel: but now there is no such appearance.

There was nothing I desired more, than that He would enlarge his kingdom, and make mine instrumental in it. Carnal reason and an ill heart their language was, Thy prayers are to no purpose; but in this strait I went to God, and begged of God for Christ's sake, that he would help me to resist my spiritual enemies: and when I was at prayer, He brought that place to my remembrance, " Though Israel be not gathered, yet is thy reward with the Lord." This was as refreshing to me, as ever my daily bread was, and put carnal reason to silence a little. But a while after, the storm rose higher; for word came, that my eldest son was dead by the way. My spiritual enemies, that have never a good tale to tell of God and his dispensations, but are often thus charging him foolishly, Why art thou to me as a liar, or as waters that fail? their language was, Thy purposes are broken off, even the thoughts of thy heart; thou thought to have had him to be a minister, but now he is dead in a strange land, and thy prayers are to no purpose. I had never such a combat with carnal reason and misbelief. I was like to lose sight of the promise which He promised me for greater things than in time. He appeared like a spirit and frightened me, as he did to the disciples. In this strait I went to God, and poured out my spirit before him; he answered me, " It is I; be not afraid." That promise was set home upon my heart with such power, " I have loved you with an everlasting love, and with lovingkindness I have drawn you;" " I entered into a covenant with thee, and thou art become mine." That is better felt, than it can be expressed, what joy it brought to me; and if weeping was in the night, joy came in the morning. Faith and love told me, I must not be discouraged at the death of my son, for Moses and Aaron died both in the wilderness, and Rachel died by the way. The saints of God were slain, and got none to bury them, and thy son got a winding-sheet and a chest of cedar-wood; and this may be a comfort to thee, that he never gave thee cause to have a sad hour for his sinful practice, though he was a captain, and with the king abroad.*

I have reason to sing of mercy and of judgment both; I hope the God whom I serve, and whose I am, has given me the life of all mine; and though he was pleased not to accept of my offer to make all my sons ministers, He has promised that he will accept of the will for the deed. And Christ, when he was upon the earth, got not all his desires answered as man : these words were set home upon my spirit, "Father, if it be possible, let this cup pass from me; nevertheless, not my will, but thy will be done." I bless God that he left this on record; for these words refreshed me much in my strait, and gave a great stroke to my spiritual enemies within. But I fear I have been too peremptory with God, in desiring to have all my sons ministers; but He knows it was his glory I designed, and the good of the Church, and I hope he has accepted my person and offer before him; for many a time I have been at God's door on their behalf, where I have been refreshed with the outlettings of his Spirit upon my soul, more than when the wicked enjoy their corn, and their oil, and their wine. It is better felt than I can express, so that I may say, All things work together for my good and advantage.

I bless God, that he hath left it on record, that a prophet was in a mistake, when he bade David go and do all that was in his heart; and a Samuel too, when he said, Surely the Lord's anointed is before him, which is my case; for He hath made choice of my youngest. If I had not the word of God, and the experience of the people of God, I had perished in my affliction; but I have reason to be hum-

* Captain William Veitch, one of the leaders and sufferers in the expedition to the Isthmus of Darien, died at sea, on his return homeward, exhausted and heart-broken with toil and disappointment.

ble and thankful, He gives me often ground to set up an Ebenezer. I thought fit to leave this on record, to encourage all mine, and all his friends and followers; for I can say, He will be found of them that seek him, and that he hath made his word sweeter to me than thousands of gold and silver. That which I have experienced of God's hearing me, may condemn all atheists, who will not believe there is a God that hears prayers, and that the Bible is the word of God; for I can say, that which I have seen, that which I have experienced, declare I unto you: I have had more pleasure in the promises, than in all the pleasures of the world.

In Dumfries there were two remarkable providences fell out;—the one was a division that happened between my husband, and his colleague Mr Patoun, and the elders, about the schoolmaster, Mr Kerr. They would have him to be precentor and session-clerk, and my husband would not consent to it, he thinking it would wrong the school; which was a great trouble to my spirit, to see the bairns of the house biting and striking one another. And I having the experience of God's hearing me by prayer, I poured out my spirit to him in prayer, that he would remove that division from amongst them. And I desire to bless His holy name for it, he granted me my petition; for they condescended to take another to be session-clerk, and so the division ended.

The other was about a great person* in this country, who summoned in some ministers and others for breaking up his gates, seeking for Popish priests: I was in great fear the Church should be wronged. I knew that God was the hearer of prayer; I went to him, that his Church might not be wronged, and he answered me with these words, He should return with shame to his own land; and it was remarkably made out, for he was necessitated to sell his coach and horses, and got not his design accomplished against the work of God; which I desire humbly to observe, and to fear,

* Earl of Nithsdale.

myself, lest I do any thing that may dishonour God. I can say it, to the commendation of free grace, that I was never in a strait, but I got help from the word of God and prayer.

One thing I cannot but observe; I think Caledonia is like a thorn in the flesh to keep me humble; I dare not say, but he made sweetness to come out of that bitter dispensation to me, for they that sow in tears, shall reap in joy. My youngest son, Ebenezer, minister at Ayr, being ordered by the Presbytery to wait upon the Commission of the General Assembly, asked liberty to come from Edinburgh to give the sacrament at Ayr, which was the last he ever gave; and after it was over, he returned to Edinburgh, where it pleased the Lord to remove him by death. When his new married wife wrote to me, that he was much out of order, it was my desire to God he would spare him, and make him more useful for him, but if he had no more service for him, he would make him both ready and willing to die; and I cannot but observe God's goodness to me, in hearing me in that, for he called for his new married wife to the bed-side, and told he would give her the parting kiss, and told her, he recommended her to his God, who had been all in all to him : and she said, " O my dear, would you not desire to stay with me, and serve God more ?" But he said, " I consult my own happiness before your pleasure, for I shall be for ever with Christ through the long ages of eternity." And he called out to some of the ministers in the room, "You passengers for glory, how near think ye I am to the New Jerusalem ?" Some answered, "Not far, Sir :" He answered, " I'll wait and climb, until I be up amongst that innumerable company of angels, and the spirits of just men." They removed his wife out of the room from him ; but when he was just expiring, she would come in again, who came running to the bed-side, but he turned her away with his hand, saying, " No more converse with the creature, I never, never, will look back again ;" so he fell asleep in Christ. It need not be a surprisal to me, for near a year before his death, he preached upon these words, "Remember, Lord, how

short my time is :" and when he was at home in his family in
Ayr, in prayer he would be so transported with the joys of
heaven, as if he would have flown away ; and his young wife
would often say to him, It was a terror to her to hear him
so much upon death; but he said it was none to him: so he
lived desired, and died lamented.

I cannot but observe the providence of God to me, for
just as the news of his death came to me, I got also the
news of my second son's arrival in England, who had been
for nine years abroad, having been a captain in the expedition to Caledonia, where so many hundreds died. And
when I met with him first at Dumfries, that word was borne
in upon me, What shall I do unto thee, O Preserver of
mankind! And from thence he went to New York, where
he married the famous Mr John Livingston's grandchild.
But that which I cannot but observe, is, that when he was
in Holland, and thereafter with King William in Flanders,
and wrote home a letter, that he was fallen sick, and, as the
doctors thought, past recovery, it was my desire to God,
he might be preserved and made useful for him. I had that
answer from God, "I change not, he shall not be consumed,
his life shall be given him for a prey in all places wherever
he goes; he shall not die, but live, and declare the works of
God." But I may say such mercies are not got but by
fasting and prayer, for, for nine or ten years I was a beggar
at God's door for the performance of those promises.

I may say from experience, he is the God of all flesh, and
there is nothing too hard for him, for he lets me know by
experience his promises can neither die nor drown ; and
yet when I meet with new difficulties, I have often my faith
a seeking, and am ready to charge him foolishly, and like
old Jacob, mourning sometimes at the supposed death of
Joseph. But he is a God that changeth not, and therefore
I am not consumed. All my desire is, that I and mine may
live in God's fear, and die in his favour, and be ready and
willing when he calls us. I may often cry out, What am
I, or my father's house, that he should so far condescend

to a piece of such sinful clay as me! But true love is above reason, for because he wills, he wills. I have reason to walk humbly all the days of my life in the bitterness of my spirit, for he hath spoken, and himself hath done it.

When the Queen sent over my son Samuel, and General Nicholson went over to take in Jamaica, she gave him a Commission to be Governor there, if he took it in. I went to God with that promise he promised to Joshua, " My presence shall be with thee, and I will never leave thee, nor forsake thee." And that in Jeremiah i. 19, " They shall fight against thee, but not prevail, for I am with thee, saith the Lord." Misbelief said, these were too great promises for me to expect the like of them, which put me many a time to God's door to seek their accomplishment: at length they yielded the place without much blood.

Afterwards she sent him with Hill and Walker, to take in Quebec; I thought it was like the taking in of Ai, and feared that there might be an Achan in the camp. I went to God for him, and got the promise, that he should not die, but live, and declare the works of God; and some of my fears came to pass, for there were six ships broken and cast away; but God was pleased to make out his promise to me, for none of the ships that he commanded were lost.

I can say from experience, They that sow in tears, 'shall reap in joy: I had more pleasure in praying for the accomplishment of the promises, than ever I had in possession: he made me know, his promise could neither die nor drown.

MEMOIRS

OF THE

LIFE

OF

MR THOMAS HOG,

MINISTER OF THE GOSPEL AT KILTEARN, IN ROSS

CONTAINING

SOME VERY SIGNAL DISPLAYS OF THE DIVINE CONDESCENSION

TO HIM, AND TO OTHERS BY HIM.

TO WHICH IS ANNEXED

AN ABSTRACT

OF

MR HOG'S MANNER OF DEALING WITH PERSONS UNDER

CONVICTION.

————————

" The secret of the Lord is with them that fear him,"—*Psal.* xxv. 14.
" Of Zion it shall be said, This and that man was born in her "—*Psal.* lxxxvii. 5.

NOTICE BY THE EDITOR.

THE "Memoirs of the Life of Mr Thomas Hog," which form the next article of biography in our collection, were originally published by "Andrew Stevenson, writer in Edinburgh," the well-known author of "the History of the Church and State of Scotland." The original edition, which is the only one that ever appeared, and which has now become exceedingly scarce, was printed at Edinburgh in the year 1756. Mr Stevenson, who takes the humble title of "the Publisher," states in his advertisement the sources, chiefly manuscript, from which he compiled these Memoirs. Had these manuscripts been extant or accessible, an original work might have been produced, richer in matter, and more regular in execution. It has, however, been found impossible even to procure the use of the scanty materials which time has left, and which, in all likelihood, will continue to exist in the form of learned lumber for some years to come. But it is not probable that any new facts in the personal history of Mr Hog could have been elicited; and the simple and pious narrative of Stevenson is perhaps, after all, the best account that could now be given of one of the most remarkable men of his age. At the same time, owing to the peculiar form into which he has thrown his materials, it may be necessary to state very briefly, the leading events in Mr Hog's life, in the order in which they occurred.

Mr Thomas Hog was born about the commencement of the year 1628, and ordained in the parish of Kiltcarn about 1654 or 1655. He was thus introduced to public service in the Church during the heat of the unhappy controversy between the Resolutioners and Protesters, occasioned by some public resolutions agreeing to the admission of persons notoriously hostile to the cause of the Reformation into places of power and trust. Mr Hog adhered to the opinions of the Protesters with such conscientiousness, that he was deposed by the Synod of Ross in 1661, because he would not decline that party judicially; but neither in this nor in any other controversy of the day, did he advocate extreme measures. In 1662, he was ejected from his charge along with many other faithful ministers, for non-submission to Prelacy. From this time he became the victim of a series of persecutions, and was not allowed to remain long in any place. In July 1668, we find him delated by the Bishop of Murray for preaching in his own house and "keeping conventicles" in Murray; on which occasion he was incarcerated for some time in Forres, till the Earl of Tweeddale procured an order to liberate him and his companions in tribulation, upon their giving bail to appear when called. Mr Hog does not seem to have desisted from the practice, so obnoxious to the tyrannical rulers of that period, of preaching the gospel wherever he found an opportunity; for in August 1675, we find letters of inter-communing issued against him among many others, by which they were driven out of the pale of society, and all were forbidden, under penalty of death, to harbour them in their houses or give them any support. And, in February 1677, the Council order Mr Thomas Hog, whom they term "a noted keeper of conventicles," to be transported from Murray to Edinburgh tolbooth. From the tolbooth, this good man was carried to the Bass, and there, at the instigation of Archbishop Sharp, thrown into the lowest and most noisome vault of that abominable prison. In October of the same year, by some influence used in his favour, he was brought back to the tolbooth, and thereafter liberated from prison, but confined to the bounds of Kintyre, under the pain of a thousand merks. Two years after, in 1679, we find him again brought to Edinburgh before the Council, again remanded to prison, and again liberated. After this, he seems to have laboured without molestation till the year 1683, when he was again dragged before the Council, charged with "house-conventicles;" and the libel being referred to his oath, and he refusing to swear, he was held as confessed, and fined in five thousand merks. He was then banished out of Scotland, and ordained to remove himself out of the country in forty-eight hours. They offered him, indeed, six weeks to provide for his banishment, if he would give bond, as some had done, not to exercise any part of his ministerial functions during that time.   He told them that, "being under much frailty of body, it was not likely he would be able; but as he had his commission from God, he would not bind up himself *one hour*, if the Lord called him and gave him strength."   So, having ordered a coach to take him up at the tolbooth door, he set off for Berwick, and from thence to London.   After remaining there for some time in great straits, he repaired to Holland, where he was introduced to the Prince of Orange, who held him in high esteem, and afterwards made him one of his chaplains.   After the Revolution, he was restored, in 1691, to his parish church at Kiltearn, as he had predicted at the time when he was ejected, thirty years before.   He died the following year, January 4. 1692, in the sixty-fourth year of his age, amidst the tears of his affectionate parishioners, who had welcomed back their aged pastor, so miraculously restored to them, after all the tossings and troubles in which the latter half of his life had been spent.   It is said, that he gave charge on his death-bed to dig his grave in the thresh-hold of his church, that his people might regard him as a sentinel placed at the door to keep out intruders.   And on his tombstone was written the following striking inscrip-tion :—

THIS . STONE . SHALL . BEAR . WITNESS .

AGAINST . THE . PARISHIONERS . OF . KILTEARN .

IF . THEY   BRING . ANE . UNGODLY . MINISTER .

IN . HERE .

Few men have lived who have been more highly esteemed by their contemporaries, or whose memory has been cherish-ed with more veneration by posterity, than the subject of the following Memoirs.   Wodrow speaks of him in his Cor-respondence, as "that great, and, I had almost said, apos-tolical servant of Christ, Mr Thomas Hog."

ADVERTISEMENT

BY THE PUBLISHER.

[MR ANDREW STEVENSON, WRITER, EDINBURGH.

THE lives of eminent saints, wherein are represented their experiences of the divine all-sufficiency, goodness, condescension, and immutable fidelity; their attainments in a holy and heavenly frame of heart and conversation, and their extensive usefulness in the various spheres to which Providence had assigned them, have been justly accounted amongst the most agreeable productions of the press. They bestow pleasure and profit, amusement and edification, at once: while the reader diverts his curiosity with the historical incidents, his mind is insensibly led into an high esteem, and emulation of that goodness by which the subject of the piece was distinguished: they set the truth and power of religion in a strong and affecting light, and may not, without reason, be regarded as additional credentials, whereby the excellency of the religion of Christ is attested and recommended anew. In them we behold what the wisest of men could not think of without astonishment, "That God does in very deed dwell with men on the earth;" nay more, dealeth familiarly with them, while he makes them previously acquainted with his secret designs both of judgment and mercy, and displays his divine power, and the efficacy of his grace, through their infirmities, subduing and conquering the most hardened obstinate sinners to himself: and while he, as it were, resigns himself to the command of their prayers, and makes them the subject of the angelic care and superintendence. Thus also the lives of the saints are perpetuated on earth, and these stars which once shone

F

in our hemisphere, though now translated to the regions of glory, yet continue their benign influence upon us.   To supply the want of these sacred intercourses, whereby Christians have been accustomed to edify one another, we hereby partake the fellowship of the saints in passages, and learn, for our spiritual improvement, the exercises of their hearts under the various dispensations of divine Providence, and their happy experiences of the Lord's care over them, and gracious manifestations of himself unto them for their encouragement, and relief from all their difficulties.

There is not any of these purposes which the Life of Mr Thomas Hog does not seem qualified to answer in an high degree.   Considered both in his private and public character, he was an ornament to religion; his doctrine and life joined to recommend the truths and ways of God to men. He had entered fully into the spirit of true godliness, and found its sufficiency for supporting all the charges of life. Hence he carried on a daily intercourse with heaven, and few enjoyed more evident expressions of the divine regard and condescension than he enjoyed.

Several passages related concerning Mr Hog are indeed of a pretty extraordinary nature :   And lest the scepticism of the present age, in relation to them, should prevail in some against the credit due to the evidence upon which the following facts are related, it is presumed to remind the reader, that as they imply nothing contrary to reason, they do not forfeit a title to his belief by being above it ; especially if they are otherways well attested, since they are obviously referred to a Cause, whose ways and thoughts are as far above the ways and thoughts of men, as the heavens are above their heads.   Nor is there a necessity of resolving such matters wholly into the inscrutable deeps of the divine sovereignty.   There are grounds laid down in Scripture for expecting great things at the hand of God : " He is able to do far above, and beyond all we can ask or think," and has positively engaged to " withhold no good thing from them that walk uprightly."   The sacred history affords us examples of a more transcendant nature than any thing here recorded, the truth of which we are at as little liberty to question, as the divinity of the Book in which they are related. And if the historical accounts left us, by Messrs Fleming, Livingston, and others, of some of these great divines, and eminent saints, the Church of Scotland has had the honour to produce, are consulted, the reader will find great numbers of more extraordinary instances than these which follow, and that so circumstantiated as to leave no room for distrusting their certainty.

The flatness in some of the familiar expressions used through these Memoirs will be found more than compensated by the ingenuousness, which discovers itself in the natural dialect of an open and overflowing heart, above any language wherewith we can possibly clothe them.

One thing more the reader is entitled to know, that the following narration is extracted from several manuscripts written by different hands, of which there are a good many copies extant ; and that every fact and principle contained therein, may be found in one or other of the following accounts, viz. :—

1. A letter by Mr William Stuart, who succeeded Mr Hog as minister of Kiltearn, and was afterwards transported to the burgh of Inverness, to the honourable Mr James Erskine, late Lord Grange. Mr Stuart's eminence and probity is yet well remembered by many. From him we have the greatest part of what may be accounted anywise extraordinary; and he declares, that he learned the same either from Mr Hog himself after his return to Kiltearn, or from old members of the Session of Kiltearn, or from William Balloch, who served Mr Hog upwards of thirty years.

2. A letter to the same Lord Grange, by way of supplement to the former, by Mr James Hog, late minister at Carnock, whose amiable character is well known. He became acquainted with Mr Thomas Hog about the year 1676, when he was brought south to stand trial for conventicles (as private meetings for worship were then nicknamed), and

they were for a time fellow-refugees in Holland. His information, which contains all that respects Mr Thomas before his ordination, with several passages of his after life, and the casuistical remarks in the appendix, were received immediately from Mr Thomas Hog's own mouth, except a particular or two, which he had from William Balloch, to whom both Mr Stuart and Mr James Hog give the character, that he was one of the most judicious, faithful, and eminent persons they ever knew of his station.

3. A letter by the said Mr James Hog to Lord Grange concerning John Card, William Balloch, &c.

4. A particular or two is borrowed from the Life of J. N. late merchant in E——h,* who was much with Mr Hog from a little after he came to the County of Murray, till near the time of his death ; but that life having, it is said, been written only for private use, we are not at liberty to be more special here.

5. Some few particulars are borrowed from the Memoirs of Mrs Ross, which are in print; and,

6. The only other authority we have access to, is a small MS. entitled, Remarkable Passages of the Life and Death of Mr Thomas Hog, &c. to which is subjoined a Letter to D. S. in Holland, subscribed by D. C., who calls himself the unworthiest of Mr Hog's converts. This, though a sort of anonymous authority, coinciding much with the other accounts, by persons of known probity, we think ourselves entitled to use it for illustrating some things which the others do but touch on.

* James Nimmo, Councillor and Treasurer of Edinburgh. Nimmo's Life forms part of the Wodrow MSS.—EDITOR.

MEMOIRS

OF THE

LIFE

OF

MR THOMAS HOG.

PERIOD FIRST.—*Containing some Gleanings of Mr Hog's Life, till he took his Degrees in the New College of Aberdeen.*

MR THOMAS HOG was born in the beginning of the year 1628, of honest parents, native Highlanders, somewhat above the vulgar rank, who lived in the burgh of Tain in the county of Ross. They were careful to give their son a liberal education; for which purpose he was early sent to school, and from his first commencement to the study of letters he discovered an uncommon genius, and soon made such proficiency as rendered him respected. During his youth he was much addicted to the harmless diversions of that age; yet they never did abate his progress in his studies, nor his detestation of every thing immoral, or unbecoming the character of a scholar.

When Mr Hog had finished his education at the grammar-school, he was put to the University in the New Town of Aberdeen, where he made great proficiency, till at last he was admitted Master of Arts, with the universal approbation of the Regents.

An incident very remarkable fell out about this time, which both confirmed Mr Hog's aversion at drunkenness,

and his belief of an overruling Providence. He had con-
tracted familiarity with a merchant in Aberdeen, who being
to go on a sea voyage, paid him a visit ere his departure;
and Mr Hog, in return of his courtesy, accompanied him to the
mouth of the River Dee, off which the ship then lay; and it
being the evening, lest the college gate, within which he
lodged, had been shut ere he returned, he took the janitor's
servant along with him. After he had seen the gentleman go
aboard, he was returning with two burgesses, who had gone
out upon the same errand; when, through the importunity
of one of them, they turned all aside to take a bottle in an
inn by the way. There he tarried with them till he thought
they had drunk sufficiently, when finding they were not yet
disposed to return home, he laid down his share of the
reckoning, and was going away. On this the company being
averse to part with him, and resolute on their cups, they
laid hold on him to detain him by force; but he being full
six feet high, and proportionably strong and vigorous, soon
twisted himself out of their grips, and went off. When he
had gone a little way, finding the porter's servant was willing to have staid longer, he gave him a little money, came
home alone to his chamber, and went to bed at his usual
hour; but though in good health, he tossed from one side to
the other, and could get no rest till after the clock struck one,
when he fell asleep, and rested quietly till his wonted time
of arising in the morning; at which time coming forth to
his class, the aforesaid servant met him, and told him with
weeping, that the two men he left yesternight, after continuing a while at their cups, fell a contending and then
afighting, in which the one killed the other; and that the
murderer being taken in hot blood, was to be tried and executed quickly. Mr Hog asked at what time the crime was
committed, and finding it was just at one o'clock, he adored
that Providence which had both disposed him to leave that
company seasonably, and made him uneasy while such a
complication of sin was committing.

The only other particular I have learned concerning Mr

Hog while at the college, is, that he having, during the study of theology, been boarded in a private house, it was his happiness to have several well-disposed young men for his comrades, with whom he joined in worship daily ; and one of them being a probationer for the ministry, he took a sort of inspection over the rest. After reading a portion of scripture, he used to propose questions and difficulties to the rest from what they had read, which proved of special use, both for their mutual information, and incitement to close study of the scriptures, and examination of commentaries, that they might be in a capacity to speak to equal advantage with their companions.

PERIOD SECOND.—*Containing some Account of Mr Hog's Conversion, and other things memorable concerning him, from the time he left the College, till he was ordained Minister at Kiltearn.*

Though Mr Hog was adorned with those natural and acquired accomplishments which constitute a truly amiable person, heightened with the lustre of an unblemished life, and strong appearances of sincere piety, he still, as himself acknowledged to Messrs Stuart and James Hog, remained a stranger to the saving operations of the Spirit of God. This, however, the divine goodness soon after made him acquainted with, at a time when the arm of the Lord was gloriously revealed in the revival of a work of reformation in this land, which commenced from the year 1638, and the influences of his grace were plentifully poured out upon multitudes through the nation. Having finished his courses of academical literature, he was called to the knowledge of things supernatural, and led into an experimental acquaintance with the great mystery of godliness. His convictions and subsequent conversion were the more endearing to him, that the innocence and apparent sanctity of his former life tended to exclude any suspicion of a bad state, and thus to strengthen him in a fatal mistake For,

1. His conversation was strictly moral : whatever is ordinarily called vice, he detested, and kept at a distance from it, and plied the duties of his station with great diligence.

2. He frequented praying societies, and conversed and prayed with them ; and in respect of knowledge, utterance, and an unexceptionable walk, he was by them esteemed a godly, well-qualified young man.

3. He sincerely sought the Lord, and was diligent in the use of means for attaining knowledge, especially of the principles of religion, and the meaning of the scriptures, as to which, his reach was greater than modesty would allow him to express.

4. With reference to the public state of religion and reformation in this Church, he was not only sound and strict, but also resolute and forward to adventure to the utmost in that cause.

5. In straits he acknowledged the Lord, and brought these difficulties before him in prayer, to which he got sometimes notable returns.

Mr James Hog having objected, That perhaps some efficacious work of saving power might have been wrought upon Mr Thomas Hog's soul more early than he believed, and that the several pieces of deportment now related, might have flowed thence ; he answered with fervent concern, That if he was then in a state of grace and salvation, he was not in that state afterward ; for that the whole of the following work, which by the Spirit and word of God was wrought on his heart, was founded upon a strong, clear, and pointed conviction of his having been at that time out of Christ, notwithstanding all the afore-mentioned lengths.

The objector desired to know how a conversation so lovely could have place without a principle of saving grace to support it ? Mr Hog replied, that there was nothing in all the particulars mentioned beyond a reformation merely legal, and that the convincing work of the Spirit held forth in John xvi. 8, 9, was yet wanting. And for detecting the objector's mistake, he observed, (1) As to a moral walk, and the performance of religious duties, there is nothing in them that demonstrates a gracious state, (Luke xviii. 10, 11, 12; Isa. lviii. 2; Rom. ii. 17–20). Neither, (2), was there any thing, said he, in his being well reputed amongst the godly, nor in that there were mutual endearments betwixt them that could confirm this charity; for his endowments of knowledge, utterance, and moral seriousness procured estimation from them, and the account they made of him, and kindness which they expressed to him, procured a reciprocation of love and kindness from him. (3.) He said, his soundness and strictness of principle was owing to the information of his judgment, by an impartial search and inquiry into principles and facts, which any man of sound understanding may attain to; and though in a time, when religion flourished, and ordinances were accompanied with much life and power, the common gifts of the Spirit did abound more than ordinary, this was not strange, as he illustrated from Heb. vi. 4, 5, 10; Psa. lxxxviii. 34; Hos. vi. 4. (4.) With reference to public zeal and resolutions, &c., there are many instances of such adventurers, who have given sad proofs of what they were at bottom, (1 Cor. xiii. 3; Matt. vii. 22, 23; Luke x. 19, 20). And (5), as to his acknowledging the Lord in prayer, and obtaining returns of prayer, he said, it was about worldly things and difficulties of that nature, which gave no evidence of everlasting love; for many such returns the body of Israel and their kings had, and the men of Nineveh were heard and delivered, (Judges ii. 15, 16; Psa. lxxviii. 38; Jonah iii. 10, &c.)

What the manner and means of Mr Hog's saving conversion were, we are at a loss to describe. In general, Mr Stuart says, after being favoured with a good part of two days' conference on that head, "That a clearer account of the work of grace could not be, than that which dropt from his lips, and this attended with so much humility and self-denial as did bear proportion to the excellency of the work;

but the particulars," says he, "would overswell my purpose." And Mr James Hog assures us, "That the issue of Mr Thomas Hog's convictions was so clear, and had so much of glory in it, that the weak vessel could scarce bear it; but, as to particulars, the only method wherein I am in case to relate them, is to repeat the ingenuous information he was pleased to give me of his own experiences, as the subject-matter of my straits required; for that great man was so far above me, who am but a mere child in grace, that it never entered into my thoughts to seek a detail of the particular circumstances and distinguishing marks of his conversion."

But in general he says, Mr Thomas Hog was under a very deep and severe law work; that his convictions were very close, particular, and pointed. His sins were set before him with much of awful majesty, which produced amazement and deep abasement on his part: that during this work, which was of long continuance, whole crowds of sins were charged home upon him without number and measure, insomuch that he concluded it would be an endless business, and was nigh to despair.

At this time he was chaplain to the Earl of Sutherland, where the work of God flourished in several happy souls. A great measure of charity was due to the Earl and several others in the family. The lady was a most eminent Christian, and of great experience in soul exercise; another lady, related to the family, was so remarkably countenanced of God, that Mr Hog came afterwards to know she was sometimes heard on his account; and the butler was at the same time under a law work much like his own, yet the one did not know of the other. Notwithstanding, the Countess wanted not, as they afterwards found, some discerning of what was working with them both, and had a watchful eye over them; and she was particularly moved to this towards Mr Hog (no doubt by her unerring Guide) on the following emergency, the only one of the kind he was ever troubled with

One time, when Mr Hog was sitting alone in his chamber, in extreme anguish, nothing but wrath in his view, and his hope of relief at a very low ebb, a horrible temptation was thrown in like a thunderbolt, viz. Why do you continue under such intolerable extremity of distress? Put rather an end to a miserable life. Immediately upon the suggestion, he resented the temptation and the tempter with indignation; and his pen-knife, at which the enemy had pointed in his suggestion, lying upon the table before him well sharpened, lest the assault should have been renewed and heightened, he rose up and threw it over the window. After this, he sat down and fell a musing upon the intricacies of his complicated distress; and while in the midst of this terrible whirlpool, the Countess, contrary to her custom (though she had been ever affable at table) knocked gently at his door, and invited him to go and partake with her of a present made her of summer fruit. So away he went with her, and though he behaved before her as if all had been quiet within, she discovered, both by her speech and her very kind behaviour, that she either was impressed with his being in danger, or that she suspected how matters were with him. After he had been thus kindly entertained for a good space, he returned to his room, found the damp mercifully removed, and his soul moulded into a more submissive frame, and disposed to wait patiently for the Lord.

As to the manner of Mr Hog's relief, we learn in general, that from a conviction of actual sins he was carried up to original sin, as the fountain-head, and to a conviction of unbelief, as the seal on this fountain, and found himself concluded in unbelief, or in a state of sin, according to Rom. xi. 32, John xvi. 8, 9, 10. The Lord having in this manner laid a solid, clear, and excellent foundation, Mr Hog was at length blessed with faith's views of the glory of Christ in his person and offices; and the light of the knowledge of the glory of God in the face of Jesus Christ, did so ravish and satiate his soul, as to render him most willing, through grace, to forego, endure, and in His strength adventure, upon any thing in his cause and for his sake.

About this time, Mr Hog having been long engaged in secret prayer, with uncommon enlargement, received so strong a confirmation of his being an object of everlasting love, from that passage in Josh. i. 5, repeated by the apostle, Heb. xiii. 5, "I will never leave thee, nor forsake thee," that his soul was filled with the consolations of God. Then, thought he, what could he want, or what harm could want do unto him, while the Lord was with him? Neither should deceit and violence prevail against him. But, while in this frame, he was longing for an opportunity of expressing his obligation to his gracious God and Saviour, and saying within himself, What would I not suffer for such unbounded goodness? That instant he was called to perform worship in the family, and went out of his room full of divine joy, expecting to pray as in his former rapture and transport; but, behold, on a sudden, he was overclouded, and deserted to that degree, that with much difficulty he got a few sentences uttered, and was obliged to cut short. When going away, the truly noble Countess whispered to him, "Mr Thomas, be not discouraged; the Lord is trying your submission to his sovereign disposure." When returned to his room, he fell a musing on his sudden change from the better to the worse; and while he was humbly inquiring why the Lord contended with him, he called to remembrance what he had upon the matter said in his secret prayer, and, as if one were reasoning with him, it was suggested, Did not you say in the time of your consolation, What would you not suffer for God? and see now ye cannot bear, without confusion, to be straightened in prayer before a few of your fellow-creatures? By this he was convinced of his weakness, and made to admire that sovereign Wisdom which took such a gentle trial of him: Upon which his confusion was removed, a pleasant submission succeeded, and his consolation was renewed. On this providence Mr Hog used to make the following observation, That submission to the sovereign will of God under desertions, afflictions, and trials, is preferable to the strongest consolations ; because, said he, "*consolation pleaseth us, but submission pleaseth God.*"

Another thing on which he puts a special remark, was a signal power and presence that attended social prayer sometimes when the Countess and her friend were present, more than on other occasions. This to carnal.minds may seem a jest; but as in natural things a threefold cord will draw more strongly than a single withe, it holds likewise in the economy of grace, that "where two or three" such believing persons shall, under the influences of the Spirit of grace, "agree to ask any thing" of their Heavenly Father, "in Christ's name, it shall be granted unto them," (Matt. xviii. 19).

But the last and most considerable adventure I shall relate concerning Mr Hog, while he abode in that noble family, was, his having been the instrument of converting a young gentleman of the name of Munro, who was related to the family and frequented it often.* This gentleman at that time, void of real religion, but of a sober deportment, took great pleasure in Mr Hog's company, and wasted much of his time with frothy, idle, and useless converse. Mr Hog had a due regard to the gentleman, and reckoned himself obliged to use him with discretion, on which account he did bear with him for a good time ; but it grieved him that these interviews turned out at best to a wasting his precious time; and therefore he took the matter to serious deliberation, and asked counsel of the Lord, what was proper for him to do in such a case. At length he was determined to deal freely with the gentleman about his eternal state : he foresaw that if his freedom were taken amiss, their converse would be broken off, and he would be eased of part of his burden ; if otherwise, then their conversation would be carried on to other and better purposes. Accordingly, an opportunity having soon presented itself, Mr Hog, after some introductory converse, and a little pause, during which he was exercised

* Mr James Hog's account.

in ejaculatory requests addressed the gentleman to this
effect, " Sir, I have a just respect to the family from which
you are descended, and to yourself also ; my parents were
acquainted with your ancestors, and I am under several ob-
ligations to them. On these and other accounts, I have
been deliberating how I may most fitly express the respect
I owe you, and, as the best service in my power, have resolved to use a piece of open-hearted freedom with you
about the concerns of your immortal soul." This unusual
address was very surprising to the gentleman, yet he took it
not in bad part, but desired him to say on. Upon this Mr
Hog proceeded, and after he had mentioned some qualities
in the gentleman, desirable in their own place, he added this
grave admonition, " Sir, I must be free with you, and therefore I tell you in sincere love, and with an ardent desire of
your soul's everlasting salvation, that you are manifestly
guilty of a notable evil ; and pray observe it carefully. It
is a transgression, or set of transgressions, that consists not
with a state of grace. ' If any man among you seemeth to
be religious, and bridleth not his tongue, but deceiveth his
own heart, this man's religion is vain,' (James i. 26),
' They have corrupted themselves, their spot is not the
spot of his children,' (Deut. xxxii. 5). The sin is, you keep
not a watch over your own tongue, but have a sort of roving conversation, not adverting to your speech, but talking at
random, and shewing no concern that God may be honoured,
and your neighbour get profit by your words. Man's tongue
is in Scripture called his glory, ' My glory rejoiceth,'
' Awake up, my glory,' (Psal. xvi. 9, and lvii. 8). Speech
we have peculiar to us as reasonable creatures, and therefore it should be savoury and useful, for every idle, inopera-
tive, or unuseful word, we shall give account at the great day."
This admonition was well supported with several texts of
scripture, particularly the two above cited ; and as an anti-
dote against this evil in time coming, Mr Hog recommended
to him to maintain the awe of the majesty of God upon his
soul ; and added he, " The presence of a prince, or a person

of respect and honour, would have so much influence upon us, as to procure some careful observance of what we say or do under his eye; and much more would a rooted faith of God's all-seeing eye prove operative in this manner." The gentleman heard all with the closest attention; and when Mr Hog had finished what he had in view, he answered, " Sir, I always looked on you as my true friend, and now you have given the best demonstration of it. By what you have said, I am persuaded of the evil of the sin charged on me, and of my danger by it ; and now that you have obliged me beyond what any have done hitherto, I beg a continuance of your favour, and that I may have free access to converse with you afterward." This request was joyfully complied with; and if the gentleman visited Mr Hog frequently before, he made him many more visits after this, but never gave occasion to impeach him. Their communication after this turned principally, and almost wholly, upon the concerns of his salvation, and, through the Lord's blessing, their labour was not in vain. The gentleman became eminently gracious; and for an evidence that this free dealing was blessed, the good man in his after conduct did so much excel in the virtues opposite to the blemishes found fault with, as astonished those who formerly knew him ; and he discovered so much understanding, deliberateness, prudence, and discretion, that he was much esteemed for accommodating differences, and several gentlemen did submit their contests to him, and acquiesced in his sole determination.

The gentleman being thus established in the Lord's way, was honoured " to adorn the doctrine of God his Saviour," without any extraordinary interruption, until a difference fell in betwixt his father and him about marriage. The old man would have him take a wife, whose portion would have relieved their little estate, then under some burden. But the young man finding no satisfying evidence of her experience of religion, would not comply; his father resented his aversion so far, that they could not live amicably together ; and to procure peace, the son was obliged to betake him to an itinerary life amongst his friends for a time, by whose intercession he hoped to make peace with the father, but in vain.

In this undesirable way the young gentleman did no small service, by stirring up several of his friends to a concern about the great salvation.

One incident which, as expressive of that just regard he had for Mr Hog, may be here inserted. It was his custom to travel much in the summer nights, that under the silence and retirement of the season, he might, with less interruption, apply himself to secret prayer, an exercise to which he was extraordinarily addicted. One of his female friends having found fault with him for this practice, as an inversion of the order of nature, an endangering of his health, and exposing himself to robbers or evil spirits; the gentleman replied, That his walking in summer nights was owing to his love of solitude, which that season afforded, without disturbance. For his health, he blessed the Lord, it was good and firm; having for some time been acquainted with a military life, the night and day in that season were nearly alike safe for his health. As to wicked men, he believed they had little encouragement to travel in the night in these parts; and as for apparitions, he could say, through grace, that he feared not devils, unless one of them were permitted to appear in the likeness of Mr Thomas Hog, for such a devil might, he said, impose upon him, and deceive him.

The order of time, according to the plan laid down, would seem to call for a stop here; but that we may have this gentleman's story all at once, we observe, That sometime after Mr Hog was ordained minister of Kiltearn, Mr Munro made him a visit, and their meeting was accompanied with very great mutual endearments. After some little time, the good man addressed himself to Mr Hog in this amazing style;—" Sir, my course is nigh finished, and I am upon my entrance into a state of eternal rest. The Lord hath his own way of giving the watchful Christian previous warning concerning the end of his warfare. 'Know-

ing that shortly I must put off this my tabernacle, even as
our Lord Jesus Christ hath shewed me,' (2 Pet. i. 14);
and I being so privileged, have been seriously pondering
where it may be most convenient to breathe out my last,
and quietly lay down this tabernacle: and seeing, after deliberation, I can find no place or company so fit as with you,
I have adventured to come and die with you."

At this time the gentleman was in good health, and ate
his meals as well as ever; wherefore Mr Hog endeavoured
to divert him from the thoughts of a present dissolution;
but he firmly persisted in maintaining his persuasion thereof,
and accordingly, in a few days, he was seized with a fever,
whereof he died.

During his sickness, Mr Hog took special care of him,
and used all the means for his recovery which the place could
afford, but without success; the fever proved mortal, yet
notwithstanding the height and violence of the disease, the
patient was never heard to rove; his concern for the honour
of God was indeed so great, that he behoved to entertain
every in-comer with some discourse suited to what he apprehended to be their case; yet so sensible was he, and had
such a reverence for Mr Hog, that he kept silence or spoke
very little when he was present, referring all to him, whom
he importuned to speak and pray often.

When the Lord's-day came, knowing that Mr Hog, who
ordinarily attended him, was engaged in the public worship
of the day, he found an errand for the person to whose care
he was committed, and in the keeper's absence, he quickly
put on his clothes, and went into the church as secretly as
he could. Ere sermon was ended, Mr Hog perceived him,
and was greatly perplexed at seeing him there; but being
ignorant what aim God might in his providence have in
bringing him thither, and persuaded that no private concerns could supersede the duty of his public calling, he pursued his discourse. Public worship being ended, the gentleman returned in all haste, and composed himself in his bed;
and when Mr Hog came into the room to inquire into the

F

dangerous adventure, he prevented him, saying, "Sir, I had the first sermon that did me good, from you, at the Earl of Sutherland's house of Dunrobin, and since that time I have had the prospect that I would get my last preaching from you also; I want no more, neither will I get more in time: and as to my bodily state, so far as I can perceive, it is just the same as before; say now whatever you please." But after this representation, Mr Hog judged that he was called to be still and reverence Providence. What was the text upon this occasion I have not learned; but Mr James Hog says, in general, that it was most suitable to the good man's case, and that he often repeated and fed upon it and the purposes delivered from it, till he entered triumphantly into the joy of his Lord.

PERIOD THIRD.—*From the time Mr Hog was ordained Minister of the Gospel at Kiltearn, till he slept in the Lord.*

Mr Hog was licensed to preach the gospel in the twenty-sixth year of his age, and ere one year elapsed, several parishes were competing for him, from some of which he might have had a greater living than ever he had at Kiltearn; but he preferred that parish to the rest, because he understood that sovereign grace was pursuing some elect vessels there, and he knew that several gentlemen in it were friends to religion, especially the Baron of Fowlis, a worthy gentleman, truly zealous for religion, as that family had been from the beginning of the Reformation.* There Mr Hog was ordained minister, in the year 1654 or 1655, with the unanimous consent and approbation of all concerned.

Mr Hog, having been thus settled, applied himself heartily to his work, taking heed to himself and to his doctrine, that he might both save himself and them that heard him.

With regard to himself, he was temperate both in diet and

* See a further account of the family of Fowlis in the Appendix to Colonel Gardiner's Life.

sleep. Gluttony, said he, is a great incentive to lust; and rising betimes is not only good for the health, but best adapted for study, wherein he had much pleasure. His more serious work, his necessary diversion, as visiting of friends and acquaintances, and even meaner things, were all gone about by rule: he kept time and measure in every thing. However lively the frame of his own soul was, he never insisted long in social duties, though he frequently enjoyed the breathings of the Holy Spirit to a very high degree. He often expressed his dissatisfaction with the length of social exercises (a fault very common amongst formal professors), as what could not be managed by many to a good account, and as encroaching upon other necessary duties belonging to our respective stations; yet he utterly disliked a coming reeking hot from the world into the presence of God, and it was his constant practice, both before and after family-worship, to retire a little into his closet. In self-examination he was very exact, and set time apart for it once a month, and sometimes oftener, accounting, that without this spiritual book-keeping, a trade with heaven could not be carried on to great advantage. Amongst his other properties, that of singular humility and modesty did excel. He was most reserved as to every thing that tended to his own reputation, and averse from speaking of such things as the Lord had wrought in him, by him, or for him, except to some few of his most entire acquaintances, or when the case of distressed souls did require it.

But he was more especially remarkable in his public character. His concern for, and sympathy with the ignorant, was exceeding great. The bulk of the people in that parish, having, through the long infirmity of their former pastor, and the intervening vacancy, been neglected in their examination, and become very ignorant, Mr Hog was at great pains to spread the catechisms, and other abstracts of our received principles amongst them; and going about from house to house, he prayed with, exhorted and instructed them in the things pertaining to the kingdom of God.

As an ambassador of the Lord Jesus Christ, his deportment was attended with as much majesty, proper to that
function, as had been observed in any; and no wonder, for
few are favoured with so many testimonies of the Divine
presence in the discharge of their ministry, as it appears he
had.   His people, says his successor,* "were awakened to
hear, and he was encouraged to preach Christ Jesus unto
them, so that the dry bones began to revive, and pleasant
blossoms and hopeful appearances displayed themselves
every where through the parish."   In like manner, after he
was forced from his charge by persecution, having come
south to Murray, and settled for a time at a place called
Knockgaudy, near Oldearn, and preached the gospel in his
private house, he was greatly owned of God, and became
the happy instrument of converting or confirming many
souls, amongst whom the same person reckons James Nimmo, and Elizabeth B——e, his spouse; B——a B——e, her
sister, afterwards Mrs S——d; Katherine Collace, alias Mrs
Ross, &c., all since fallen asleep.   The same Mr Nimmo
observes concerning Mr Hog,† "That though the Lord did
not bless Mr Hog with children, he once gave him the
powerful assurance of that promise, 'I will give thee a name
better than of sons and daughters,' (Isa. lvi. 5); which he
signally fulfilled to him, in making him the instrument of
begetting many sons and daughters to the Lord; to do
which the Lord assisted him more I judge than any in his
day."   Mrs Ross also gives a large testimony to the success
of Mr Hog's ministry in the Memoirs of her life.   When
speaking‡ of Satan's being let loose upon her with his
temptations, by which her hope was almost vanquished;
" The Lord," says she, " sent Mr Thomas Hog, 'an inter-
preter, one of a thousand,' who was directed to put me upon
a right way of recovery, and quieting my mind under present trouble, which was, *when I could not resist temptation,
to suppose all true that Satan could charge me with, and
then make application to the blood of Jesus, that cleanseth*

---

* Mr Stuart.   † Memoirs of his own Life.   ‡ Page 15.

from all sin; and he taking me to his house, where I staid for the space of a month, the Lord thoroughly restored my soul before I returned." Again, speaking of Mr Hog's liberation from prison (which I learn elsewhere was first at Forres), she says,* "He preaching for eight years thereafter in his own house, was the instrument of converting many, and ministers about did also wax bold by his example to fall about the work of preaching." And to carry this account down to the latter period of his life, " I have," says Mr James Hog, " had the desirable occupation to hear him preach at the Hague, and his sermons were accompanied with the greatest measure of life and power I have ever had the opportunity to observe in my poor life.—This is he," says the writer of the remarkable passage, " of whom I may truly, and without disparagement to any, say, that he was the father of the most eminent, as well ministers as private Christians, in the land, viz. the famous and judicious John Munro, in Ross, who had been before a great enemy to him, but at length was by his labours begotten unto God; also, the learned and faithful Mr Thomas Taylor had a most deep, distinct, and long exercise under Mr Hog's ministry, and in the end got a clear and safe out-gate, and was thereafter an eminent and shining light both in Scotland and Ireland.—As also, that brand plucked out of the burning, Mr Angus Macbean, minister at Inverness: the Lord had indeed begun to work upon Mr Macbean, and brought him out from among the curates before he saw Mr Hog in the face, but he never had any distinctness in his exercise, far less outgate from his trouble, till the Lord brought him to this eminent seer, who, by converse and otherwise, was the instrument of opening his eyes, and of drawing him most effectually to Christ, after he had been about four years under a deep and heavy exercise of law-work. But time would fail me to speak of the strength, settlement, and establishment in grace, and in the ways of God, that holy Mr Thomas Ross, and zealous Mr John Welwood, together with several others,

* Page 65.

did get by his ministry and means, and of the many eminent Christians in every place to which the Lord called and sent him, who were converted or confirmed by his ministry."

As a further evidence of that special conduct vouchsafed to Mr Hog in the dispensing of gospel ordinances, it was remarkable, that he was several times led to speak particularly to persons and cases, without any foreknowledge of the special occasions calling for it. One time, William Balloch, his faithful servant, whom the Lord had powerfully brought over from darkness to light by his ministry, was seized with a fever; and, in that condition, the tempter endeavoured by several specious arguments to deprive him of his peace. By this he was made almost insensible to bodily distress; and for relief he adventured to scramble up stairs upon his hands and feet, that he might impart his difficulties to his master; but Mr Hog being to preach in a short space after, refused to speak with him at that time; so with great difficulty he returned to his bed, and in a little he found that God had provided for his relief. As Mr Hog preached in his dwelling-house, William's bed was so situated that he could hear his master distinctly, and was surprised to find himself prevented as to all he had to impart; for each of the several temptations, which pressed him so exceedingly, were distinctly mentioned, and the fallacies detected in the sermon. Thus the Lord, by his own ordinance, made known to his poor servant all that was in his heart; and in that manner a happy cure was bestowed on his soul, which issued in the recovery of his health.*

In like manner one Christian Macintosh, a poor woman, in the depths of soul distress, having several times gone to hear Mr Hog at a good distance from her house, and staid in his house sometimes two or three nights at a time; some of her acquaintances took the opportunity one night in their way home, to reprehend her for being absent from her family, because it might provoke her husband, who was of a different mind from her, and be an occasion of blackening

* Mr J. H. g's account

religion itself, as if it gave a handle to idleness. With this, and more to the like purpose, the poor woman was exceedingly affected. She replied with great humility, that the worthy minister had detained her, that the entanglements she was under about her soul-concerns might be the more easily removed; and that his instructions had been of great use for this purpose: that her family was small, and the business of it could be the more easily overtaken, or what was wanting made up more conveniently, when matters of higher importance were brought to some desirable issue. After parting to their several abodes, Christian stopped at a retired place in her way, where she poured out her heart to the Lord, and at her return home, her husband received her with the most tender affection. Of all this Mr Hog knew nothing, yet the very next Lord's day he was led to preach from these words in Matt. xxvi. 10, " Why trouble ye the woman? for she hath wrought a good work upon me ;" and in handling the same, to obviate every objection, which Christian's honest friends had, from no evil design, made use of; which wrought so with them, that they all acknowledged their mistake to her, and when it pleased the Lord further to establish her, the occasion for such umbrage ceased.*

To instance only one particular more of the kind : Munro of Lumlair, an heritor in the parish, having been guilty of some sin wherewith it seems his own conscience accused him, fell to applying some reprehensory expressions uttered by Mr Hog, as if designed for exposing him to contempt, though Mr Hog had no eye to him ; and being incensed to a dreadful degree, he came to the Session to demand satisfaction of Mr Hog ; otherwise he threatened, not only to withdraw himself and family from his ministry, but to lay his strictest commands upon his tenants to do so likewise. Mr Hog heard all without interrupting the gentleman ; and then addressed the Session, of which the gentleman's chief, Sir John Munro of Fowlis, was a member, unfolding the in-

* or Jean Hog's account.

sult in most weighty and significant terms, and required
them to take cognizance of the scandal; and lest it should
have been alleged, any of the members would be influenced by
his continuance with them, he retired to his closet. After Mr
Hog's departure, Sir John accosted his friend, and by threats
(as he was of the greatest authority in the place) and arguments together, he prevailed with him ere they parted, to
come in the minister's will. Mr Hog was ready to overlool
what respected himself personally; but the ministerial office
being attacked, and the offence become flagrant, the Session
ordered that Lumlair should be rebuked in his seat the next
Lord's day; to which he submitted, and made his confession
with many tears, to the affecting of the congregation. Nor
was the gentleman's penitence confined to that occasion,
but he ever after looked on Mr Hog as his best friend, and
laid out himself to great purpose, to promote the success of
his ministry.*

So soon as it pleased the Lord to bless Mr Hog's paro-
chial labours with a gracious change wrought upon a considerable number of the people, he took care to join the
more judicious amongst them in a society for prayer and
conference; these he kept under his own special inspection,
and did heartily concur with, and assist them in, exciting
and edifying one another.

In prayer he was most solemn and fervent; the profoundest reverence, the lowest submission, and yet a marvellous boldness and intimacy with God, attended his engagements in this exercise. It might be truly said of him,
as of Luther, When he prayed, it was *tanta reverentia, ut
si Deo, et tanta fiducia, ut si amico,*—"with as much reverence as if he were speaking to God, and with as much
boldness as if he had been speaking to his friend." The
strength of his faith was proof against discouragement;
none ever beheld him perplexed on account of difficulties.
Having once committed his cause unto the Lord, he could
wait with assurance of a happy event; and he obtained

* Mr James Hog's account.

many remarkable and even extraordinary returns, of which several instances shall be here taken from the author of the Remarkable Passages, and Mr James Hog's account; such as,

1. A good woman having come to Mr Hog with a sore lamentation that her daughter, C—— L——, was distracted, Mr Hog charged one or two devout persons (for he frequently employed them on extraordinary occasions) to set apart a day and night for fasting and prayer, and then to join with him in prayer for the maid the next day. Accordingly, when the time of their appointment for a joint concurrence in the duty came, he wrestled for the distressed person till she recovered her senses, and became as quiet as ever she was before. This the writer declares he knew.

2. A daughter of the Laird of Parks, his brother-in-law, being lodged with him, and being seized with a high fever, and little hope of life left, Mr Hog, who loved the child dearly, consulted with his wife whether there was any cause, either in him or her, of the Lord's contending with their friend while under their care; and acknowledging their offences jointly to the Lord in prayer, with the iniquity of the child, the fever instantly left her, and she was restored to health. This passage, says the writer, I read in Mr Hog's diary, which he concludes with admiration of the mercy and condescendence of his good and gracious God, to whom he ascribes the praise of all.

3. In like manner, a child of the Rev. Mr Thomas Urquhart having been at the very point of death, those present pressed Mr Hog to pray (for he was now become so revered, that none other would, in such cases, pray when he was present); upon which he solemnly charged them to join fervently with him; and having wrestled in prayer and supplication for some time, the child was restored to health. A like instance is found in his diary, with respect to a child of Kinmundy.

4. One David Dunbar, who lived at a distance, being in a phrenzy, and coming to Mr Hog's house in one of his roving fits, Mr Hog caused him to sit down; and having

advised with Mr Fraser of Brae, and some other persons who were occasionally present, what could be done for the lad, some were of opinion that blood should be drawn of him; but, said Mr Hog, the prelates have deprived us of money wherewith to pay physicians, therefore we will make use of the Physician who cures freely, and so he laid it on Brae to pray; but Brae having put it back on himself, he commanded the distracted man, in a very solemn awful manner, to be still; after which he prayed most fervently for the poor man, and he was immediately restored to his right wits. This, says the writer, I both read in his diary, and had from eye and ear witnesses.

5. Mr Hog having gone once to see a gracious woman in great extremity, and sad distress both of body and mind, he prayed with and for her; and in prayer he had this remarkable expression among many others, " O Lord, rebuke this tentation, and we, in thy name, rebuke the same." Immediately after which, the person (as she told the writer of these passages) was restored to entire health both of body and mind.

And yet notwithstanding the Lord honoured him so eminently, it is doubtful if any in his day did more heartily detest and carefully guard others against delusion than he did; ordinarily, when he bowed his knee, it was his fervent request to be saved from delusion, and therefore, when any word of scripture was brought to his mind, as suiting any case he was exercised about, he would not close with it, till, after much fervent supplication, and diligent inquiry in the use of all suitable means, he had examined the same, and found it from God; for, said he, Satan comes many times with his temptations as an angel of light.—Wherefore it was his constant judgment, wherewith his practice agreed, that as it is only by the word wherein is clear light, and by the Spirit's opening the eyes and giving sight to discern this light, that we are to expect any solid instruction, direction, or comfort. To where these two concur, there is satisfying evidence of our light coming from the

Lord. There is first light in the understanding, which works on the will, and the affections follow. The spirit of truth acts like himself in a gentle, sweet, sure, sanctifying, humbling, and quieting manner.

But passing this: amongst the means which Mr Hog used for the good of the people, the following method was much countenanced of God. He set time apart to converse fully and freely with those who sought the privilege of baptism to their children; and, if he found them ignorant of the nature and ends of that sacrament, he was at as great pains to bring them to repentance and reformation, as if they had been really scandalous, and kept them from the benefit of baptism till he discovered a change on them to the better. Of the marvellous use of this course several instances might be given, but one may serve at present, and a most remarkable one it is.*

There was in this parish a bold young fellow, John Munro, *alias* Card, so called from his occupation, being a tinker by trade, to distinguish him from the other Munros with whom that country abounds. This man, who loved to give and take his bottle, and was accounted witty and facetious, happened to have a child to baptize; but accounting Mr Hog too rigid in his examination, he had no will to go to him; but go he must, for the discipline of the Church in those days permitted no man to go without the bounds of his own parish for baptism, without a license from his minister, which did mightily strengthen the authority of ministers. So John Card being shut up in this dilemma, either to want baptism to his child, or go to his minister, at length resolves upon the latter. Mr Hog received him courteously, and knowing his errand, took him apart and examined him, but finding him unqualified to receive that seal of the covenant, he told him so much in plain language, and gave him his best advice to agree with God, " while he was in the way" of life; and recommended to him to get the Assembly's Shorter Catechism by heart, and to come next week to give

* From Mr Stuart's account.

account of his success.　John goes home, but being as yet
insensible of his mercy, was in no haste to comply with the
advice given him, nor to return to his minister at the time
appointed ; however, the case straitened him, and therefore
return he must once more, and he was resolved it should be
but once.　So he comes again to his minister, and in an in-
sulting manner asks him, how long he would be so cruel as to
keep his child from baptism ?　Mr Hog answered him with
meekness, that the cruelty was on his own side, who was
at no pains for his salvation, and the salvation of his child ;
and added, " If I should administer baptism to your child
without warning you of your hazard, I should be more
cruel than you, for you would perish in your iniquity, and
God would require your blood at my hands."　To enforce
the reproof, Mr Hog asked some questions concerning the
nature of sin and wrath ; but John fretted therewith, said,
in a peremptory manner, " Well, minister, will you give me
baptism to my child or not ?" and Mr Hog answering, " the
Lord's time is the best time ; when you are fitter to receive
that privilege, I shall be more willing to grant it."　John
was angry, and said, " Well, sir, keep it to yourself, you'll
give me baptism when I ask it again, farewell."　And so
he went off in a huff.

But by the time John Card reached his own house, he
found great uneasiness in his mind.　The thoughts of what
Mr Hog represented to him did pursue him, and particularly
what he said concerning sin, wrath to come, and the necessity of being reconciled to God.　When night came he
went to bed as usual, but could not sleep, his thoughts
troubled him ; so up he arose, and set about prayer, a duty to
which he was a very great stranger, and finding his distress to
grow, he goes next day to the minister.　Mr Hog knowing
the haughtiness of the man's spirit, was surprised to see him
come so soon back, yet he received him kindly, and asked
what brought him to-day ?　The other answered that he had
had no rest in his mind since he was with him ; that he was
followed, as with a familiar spirit, with the thoughts of God's

wrath against him for sin; and was so full of ignorance of
God, and of sin and duty, heaven and hell, that he could
form no right judgment concerning them.   Upon this information, Mr Hog instructed him at great length concerning the important subjects aboved named, and then prayed
with him; and finding remarkable assistance vouchsafed
to him in both these duties, and having otherwise an excellent discerning of the gracious operations of the Spirit of
grace, he gave the man such directions as he judged proper
for a person in his condition, and desired him to bring forward his child for baptism with the first opportunity; for
now (said he) I hope God hath begun to convince you of
sin and misery, and will, in his own good time, discover the
remedy unto you.   But John refused to do this as peremp-
torily, as before he had requested for the benefit of it; and
being filled with a sense of his rebellion against God, he
added, " No, no; no baptism for me, I have no right to it;
nothing is due to me but hell and damnation."   Mr Hog
still urged him to bring forward his child, but he would not
be prevailed on to do so, and away he went in tears, re-
questing the minister to continue his prayers, if peradventure
God would have mercy on him.   A work of conviction continued with this man, which was found to be real, clear and
permanent.   Mr Hog, whose concern for him was very
great, found the work of grace advancing most sweetly in
his soul; yet all this time his mind was not calmed, his dis-
quiet continued for several months after, when, to his sweet
experience and exceeding joy, the hand which wounded him
did also heal him, which happened as follows.

Upon a certain Lord's day, John Card arose early, and
his cries unto God vied with the dawning of the morning.
In this prayer he got such a sight of sin, as filled him with
great abasement; and he was made to cry to God for
mercy, with all the arguments he could form; and gave not
over till he obtained a glimpse of nope, that God would
have mercy on him; yet in a little the former load on his
spirit recoiled upon him.   When he came to church, he

found more uneasiness than he expected. Atheism and heart plagues did fiercely assault him, and he was afraid lest he should perish by them; but to his great surprise, the hour came, when his dead soul was made to hear words of eternal life. The minister was directed to preach Christ so clearly to his very soul, that he found it a time of love, and a day of salvation, so that he was in a very transport of joy; and after the first sermon, he comes to the minister's closet door, which, contrary to his custom at other times, he had forgotten to bolt at that time; so in the man comes, and though he found worthy Mr Hog on his knees, such was honest John's transport, for now I may call him honest, that he cried, " Mr Thomas, O Mr Thomas, turn your prayers to praises on my account, for this day salvation is come to my soul." Mr Hog was amazed to find any giving him disturbance in time of secret prayer; but cut short, as if he had been at a close; and being wise and composed he did conceal his surprise, and examine the other gravely and composedly, and found a most comfortable and satisfying account of the impression made by that sermon upon his mind, will, and affections, viz. upon his mind, while the minister was representing the glory of Christ, and how wonderfully well fitted he is for the salvation of sinners. " God who commanded the light to shine out of darkness shined on his soul, giving him the knowledge of the glory of God in the face of Jesus Christ," which turned his will to the acceptance of the Saviour, and to resign himself to him on his own terms; upon which he found his soul filled with wonder, joy, and peace unspeakable. Of the truth and ingenuousness of this account, Mr Hog was very well satisfied, and, according to John Card's request, he turned his prayers into praises on his account; and good reason he had for doing so, for this man proved one of the most remarkable converts in this country, or perhaps in the kingdom, and continued to adorn the doctrine of God his Saviour to the end of his life, which was not for many years after this. And it was observable in him, that he carried a great resemblance of Mr Hog ever after, in a solid discerning of persons and spirits in matters of religion, as it was in several other worthy persons, who acknowledged Mr Hog as their spiritual father in Christ Jesus. "I had," says Mr James Hog, "the happiness to see him twice or thrice, and to converse a considerable while with him by the means of the reverend Mr William Stuart, minister of Inverness, who interpreted for us both; and I must say, that except the great Mr Thomas Hog, no person ever tried me, and went so much to the very bottom of my heart, as he was directed to do, both as to the ground-work, and the most important concerns of a Christian life. He was then of a great age, not many years under a hundred, and though very frail in body, yet fully ripe in understanding, memory, and other soul faculties, and advanced in saving grace to a prodigy. While conversing with him I thought I was as it were at the feet of one of the old prophets, for besides a wonderful penetrating reach, his aspect was full of majesty and gravity."

As Mr Hog's care was great in admission to the sacrament of baptism, he was fully more strict in his admission to the sacrament of the supper, which was the reason he did not dispense that ordinance for several years after he was settled minister at Kiltearn. He had indeed the profoundest regard for that solemnity, and would most gladly have had it sooner; but the ignorance of the people was so great when he entered amongst them, that it was long ere they were in any readiness to receive it: but when he had been about four years in the ministry, and observed that his labours were countenanced of the Lord, he set about preparation for that holy ordinance, and proceeded with the greatest caution, allowing none to communicate who could not give some tolerable satisfying account of a work of grace upon their souls.* And having thus fenced that solemn ordi-

* Happy were it for the present generation, if ministers would universally tread this step of the eminent Mr Hog. By "separating," in this manner, "betwixt the precious and the vile," they would give evi-

nance, great was the encouragement found in it : severals
told him how graciously God had dealt with their souls,
both before and after the communion. " I cannot (says
Mr Stuart, from whom I am now gleaning) give account of particulars, but I have heard some eminent
Christians, who were present at that occasion, tell, that
' the Lord bowed his heavens and came down,' and displayed his saving power on that occasion most comfortably and signally; and I (says the same reverend minister)
found a still more persuasive evidence of the efficacy of
that solemnity remaining forty years after it. In the year
1699 or 1700, when I was minister of Kiltearn, Donald
Munro, the oldest man in the parish, fell sick, and died.
He was 96 years of age, and lived two miles from the church,
yet he attended there punctually every Sabbath. His conversation was very agreeable, but he was not reckoned
amongst either the first or second rate of Christians for profession or power of religion. When I heard of his sickness,
I went to visit him, and being somewhat weary with walking,
I sat down softly at some little distance from the sick man,
without letting him know that I was there, and in a little
time I heard him pronounce these words, ' Remember my
death till I come again ;' and these he repeated three or
four times, and his affections were so moved with them,
that he broke out in tears. At first I suspected that might
be the effects of sickness or old age, but to my great joy, I
was soon undeceived, for when I drew near, and asked him
what death is that you speak of, and repeat so often ? he,

dence of their divine mission, and in doing so, they would at least
save their own souls from accession to others' guilt; whereas, by ad-
mitting too many, who, to say the best of them, shew only negative
qualifications, they not only partake of other men's sins, but are guilty
of leavening those with it who join them; whereby, on the one hand,
they grieve the hearts of the gracious, and provoke them to make a
schism in the body; and on the other, harden the impenitent, make the
offering of the Lord to be abhorred, and, which puts the copestone on
all, provoke the holy Lord to jealousy with their remissness. What
the issue of this procedure must be, he that runs may read. [*Note by
the Original Publisher.*]

turning towards me, said, with a lively voice, and pleasant
countenance, " The death through which I look for victory
over a body of sin and death; the death that supports me
in this dark valley and shadow of death; the death through
which I look for eternal life; the death of Jesus Christ the
Prince of life,—that, sir, is the death of which I speak."
Being much refreshed with this answer, I asked him, how
he came by the sense of eternal mercy through the death of
Christ? He answered me with much warmth of affection,
that when Mr Hog gave the sacrament, above forty years
ago, he preached on the death of Christ, and the infinite
virtue of it for poor sinners, which filled him with such wonder and joy at the love of Christ, as made Him precious to
his soul above all things in time and eternity; and though
he lost the sense of it for many years, that it had now re-
curred with such vigour, as if he had heard it with the
same power that moment. I received several other comfortable answers from him, and then asked if he would
have me pray; to which, without answering me, he looked
up, and with great emotion said, ' O Lord, be pleased to
hear this prayer.' And in a short time after I had prayed,
he resigned his soul to God, in a pleasant assurance of eternal life through Christ."

Mr Hog seems not to have administered the holy supper
again while he was at Kiltearn, for when after he had retired to Knockgoudy, finding his ministry in private blessed
with success, he gave that sacrament for the second time,*
which was a bold attempt, considering the severity of the
laws against them; nevertheless several of the most exercised in godliness in these parts attended that solemnity,
which was remarkably countenanced with the divine presence and glory: communicants returned to their habita-
tions with joy unspeakable, and the spirits of their adversaries were so bound up that they gave them no disturbance.

Amongst the things reckoned extraordinary on this occasion, the admission of a Highlander, who could speak no

* Mr Stuart's account.

G

English, is accounted worthy of a place both in Mr Stuart's
and Mr Hog's accounts. This man, John MacLeod by
name, known to Mr Thomas Hog as a man sweetly exercised
in religion, and by whom others say they were afterward
greatly refreshed, had come up from Ross-shire to that solemnity, and wanted to communicate, but because Mr Hog
knew he had no English, he hesitated to admit him. Here-
upon, the good man being very intent on communicating,
and knowing that Mr Hog had the Irish language, says to
him in that dialect, " Would ye stop me, who came hither
obeying the command of my exalted Redeemer, and who
understand what you was just now preaching in English so
well as if every word had been delivered in my own tongue."
And thereupon he repeated the substance of the discourse
that had been delivered. This having been interpreted by
Mr Hog to those who were present, filled them with wonder, and the good man was allowed to communicate, which
he did with great joy.

But as God sent Mr Hog to be an ambassador of mercy
to many, so also to be a messenger of wrath to some. Of
this several instances are related;* and I shall repeat the
following. About the beginning of Mr Hog's ministry, a
certain gentleman in the parish having lost one of his family, intended to bury within the kirk; but because, on
account of the vulgar superstition, the General Assembly
had made an act against burying in churches, and that Mr
Hog was a strenuous defender of the acts of the Church,
the gentleman was at a nonplus what to do: upon which,
one William Munro, a strong hectoring fellow, engaged to
the gentleman to make good his way against all opposition,
and had succeeded so far, that the people who attended the
corpse were entering the church-yard, when Mr Hog, getting notice, went out, and setting his back to a door, through
which the corpse was to be carried, began to reason with
the people, to convince them of the error of breaking through
good order, and the rules of the Church. This had not,

* By Mr Stuart, &c.

however, the desired effect on all, for the fellow who had
occasioned this disturbance laid violent hands on Mr Hog,
to pull him from the door; but Mr Hog, having the spirit
of a man as well as of a Christian, turned on his adversary,
wrested the key out of his hand, and having told the as-
sailant, that were he to repel force with force, probably he
would be no gainer, he did next speak to the people, saying, " This man hath grieved the Spirit of God, and you
shall see either his sudden repentance, or a signal judgment
befal him." Accordingly, the poor wretch continuing in his
wicked courses, met with the judgment foretold him in a few
months after, and a very signal judgment it was; for he,
having in one of his drunken revels made a violent attack
upon a mean man, and thrown him into the fire, the man,
in his extremity, drew out the wretch's own sword or dagger, and therewith thrust him through the belly, so that his
bowels burst out, and he expired most miserably.

A second instance of this kind happened while Mr Thomas
Hog was lecturing one evening in the house of the Laird
of Lethem, in the county of Murray.* During the time of
worship he observed a servant laugh once and again; the
first time he gently called for attention and reverence, and
at the second transgression he rebuked what he saw more
severely, and then went on in his purpose with great composure; but a little after, observing the same person relapse
into his contemptuous carriage, he paused for some time, and
then said with an air of awful severity, " The Spirit of God
is grieved by one of the company, for mocking at these
great truths: therefore, I am bold to say, such offers of
grace shall be visibly and more suddenly punished, than
any here would wish, and that the guilty person would give
much for our prayers when he cannot have them." After
the family had supped, and retired to their several apart-
ments, a message came to Mr Hog's chamber, telling him
that the foresaid mocker was suddenly seized with violent
sickness, and that he cried bitterly for him. Upon this, Mr

* From Mr Stuart's and Mr Hog's account.

Hog arose quickly, cast on his night-gown, and came down stairs to see him, without losing a minute's time, but before ever he came, the poor creature was dead.

These awful providences did very justly fill the hearers with the fear of God's judgments, and confirmed many of them in the belief, that the secret of the Lord was with Mr Hog, which was also verified by many other evidences.

The two following instances* are of still greater consequence. In the year 1685, when the Duke of Monmouth landed in England, and the Earl of Argyll in Scotland, Mr Hog being then in London, his servant brought him in the news of their landing, expecting that it would be very acceptable to his master, but he was disappointed; Mr Hog shook his head, and William Balloch adding, " O, Sir, what is the matter? honest people were under dreadful apprehensions of popery coming in amongst us like a deluge, and now they hope these two great men may be the happy instruments of delivering those nations." Mr Hog knowing him to be a gracious man, and that he was prudent, and might be confided in, said, " I tell you, man, God will not honour any of these men to be the instruments of our deliverance, and I have good reason to think so as to both; for when some worthy patriots who saw the danger of popery, and what danger king Charles was in from popish councils, met together, in order to confer about the properest measures to be taken in these circumstances, Monmouth, who was in the concert, declined to act the honourable part which fell to his share, upon which all measures broke up, and some of the worthiest in the land were exposed to suffering on that account ; and because he would not embrace the Lord's time of working, God will not accept of his time. And as for the Earl of Argyll, I believe he is a good man, and that he will get his soul for a prey; yet, considering his hand hath been deep in the defection and apostasy of the time, I am under no expectation of deliverance by him."

Much about the same time some Protestants, who attend-

* Taken from Mr Stuart.

ed the court, knowing that Mr Hog was in the city, and that he was endued with somewhat of a prophetic spirit, spoke liberally of him at court, which drew King James's attention so far, that he wanted Mr Hog should be consulted concerning the state of affairs at that juncture. This being communicated to Mr Hog by his friends, he concealed his mind for some time, till he had consulted the Lord in prayer, and prepared for his departure thence, and then he complied with their importunity, and told them (what also he charged them to report faithfully,) " That if King James had sincerely adhered to the principles of our holy reformed religion, his throne had been established in righteousness; yea, if his majesty would yet give sincere evidence of his turning from popery, matters might be well with him; but if he did it not suddenly, and sincerely, the land would spew him out." This answer having been faithfully reported to the king, orders were quickly issued out to apprehend Mr Hog, and a strict search was made for him, but he, having foreseen this evil, eschewed it by a speedy flight to Holland.

Nor was Mr Hog's prophetic spirit confined only to things on the dark side of the cloud; some events of mercy were also foretold by him,* such as,

1. When he knew that he was to be put out of his charge at Kiltearn, anno 1662, (as the most of our faithful ministers were put out of theirs much about the same time,) he had a farewell sermon to them, in which he took God and their own consciences to witness, that he had not shunned to declare to them the whole counsel of God, and that he had foretold them the things they now saw coming. He further told them, *That the storm would be of long continuance, but after all, the sky would clear, and he would live to see it, and be called to his own charge again as minister of Kiltearn, and die with them.* " The truth of this I had attested to me (says Mr Stuart) by several old men in the parish, who were my Elders." And added Mr Hog, " If

* From Mr Stuart.

any of you shall decline from that good way, and these truths wherein ye have been taught, and shall comply with the wicked designs now carried on, *I take heaven and earth to be witnesses against you; I take the stones of these walls I preach in, every word that was spoken, and every one of you to be witnesses against another."* With these, and many other words, he warned and exhorted them, and his labour was not in vain, for there was not a parish in Scotland which complied less with the corruptions and defections of the time than his did.

The only other instance I shall name of the kind, was his predicting the glorious deliverance at the Revolution, by the means of the Prince of Orange. When he foretold that miscarriage of Monmouth and Argyll, he added, " Yet I am under apprehensions that our deliverance is reserved for another happy instrument of the divine glory." And when he went to Holland, he was soon introduced to the Prince of Orange, who had him in great esteem for his singular piety and prudence, and therefore he took him into the secret of his resolutions to do what he could to deliver these nations from popery and tyranny; in which that good man being desired to declare his sedate thoughts, and most deliberate sentiments, encouraged his Highness perhaps as much as any who ever spoke to him upon the head, upon topics of revelation and experience; and assured him, if he undertook the great work of delivering these nations from Popery, and of securing the Protestant religion, with a sincere eye to the glory of God, the Lord would be with him, and make him successful, for he had the strongest impressions that his Highness would be the happy instrument of Providence in that deliverance.*

Yet, notwithstanding this extraordinary gift became thus familiar to Mr Hog, he was exceeding cautious about it, and afraid of an itching desire after it. Blind impulses, violent, sudden, and unreasonable injections, he could not away with, but many times testified against them; as also

* Mr Stuart's account.

against light by dreams, visions, and voices, or any such
signs, as an adulterous generation, going a whoring from
God and the more sure word of prophecy, do seek after;
and therefore it was his custom to examine these much in
the same way he did the answers to his prayers, which we
formerly noticed.

The interpositions of the providence of God for this his
gracious servant, in the time of his extremity, are also very
remarkable, and deserve a special *memento*.

The first time Mr Hog was imprisoned for the truth was
at Forres, anno 1668, upon a complaint for keeping conventicles, &c. There he was wonderfully strengthened and
comforted, and had great joy in his sufferings. The godly
who knew him, or heard of him, were also incessant at a
throne of grace on his account; and several, experienced
in religion, amongst which number Mrs Ross was one, declared afterward, that they never saw, or at any time found,
such a measure of the spirit of supplication as was then
poured out on many in Moray; and their prayers, as one
saith of the Church's prayers for Peter while in a like case,
"set God a-working." The effect was, that Mr Hog, without his own knowledge, and most unexpectedly of all his
friends, was set at liberty without any concessions on his
part.

A second instance of this kind is yet more remarkable.*
Mr Hog having, about the beginning of the year 1676, been
again apprehended for private conventicles, and sent up to
Edinburgh, he said to some persons in company, " I thank
my God, this messenger was most welcome to me;" and
giving a scratch with his nail upon the wall, he said, " I
trust in the living God, that before my conscience shall get
that much of a scratch, this neck (pointing to it) shall go
for it." Accordingly, when put to the trial, he joyfully
submitted to a prison, rather than bind up himself from
preaching, and was therefore sent to the Bass, where his
Christian carriage and conversation, composure, courage,

* Mr Stuart's and Mr James Hog's accounts.

and pleasantness of spirit, proved very comfortable to the
other suffering ministers there. However, the air of the
place, and close confinement, affected his health very soon,
and he fell into a bloody flux, which, in his case, was attended with peculiar and very great danger. In this situation, a physician was called to his assistance from Edinburgh, who gave it as his opinion, that unless he was liberated from that confinement, there was no hope of his recovery; and he advised him to supplicate the council for
liberation for some short space, that means might be used
for the recovering of his health. Mr Hog hesitated to address them; whether because they were a mongrel court,
consisting of clergymen as well as laymen, or because he
judged they had no right to deny what he asked, or because he had no prospect of succeeding, is uncertain. However, the doctor, of his own accord, and without owning
Mr Hog in it, drew up a petition for him to the council, in
the strongest terms he could devise; and the better to en-
sure a hearing, the clerk's dues were liberally paid. The
petition was read, and some of the lay lords interceded for
Mr Hog, and said, while he was at liberty he lived more
quietly, and traversed not the country so much as other
Presbyterians did. Upon which, Archbishop Sharp, taking
up the argument, said, That the prisoner did, and was in a
capacity to do, more hurt to their interests, sitting in his
elbow chair, than twenty others could do by travelling from
this land to the other; and if the justice of God was pursuing him to take him off the stage, the clemency of the
government should not interpose to hinder it; and therefore it was his opinion, that if there were any place in the prison
worse than another, he should be put there. This motion
having been seconded by some other of the prelates and
their supports, was accordingly put to the vote, and it carried, *The closest prison in the Bass for him;* which was
speedily put in execution. When the keeper intimated
the order, Mr Hog raised himself up, with some difficulty,
in his bed to read the sentence, "which," said he, "was as

severe as if Satan himself had penned it." William Balloch, his servant, being with him when he was carried down to a low nasty dungeon in the Bass, fell a-weeping, and cried, "Now, master, your death is unavoidable." Upon this, the good man's eyes were directed to the Lord as his physician, and turning to his servant, with a countenance full of joy, he said, "Now that men have no mercy, the Lord will shew himself merciful; from the moment of my entering this dungeon, I date my recovery." And so it fell out, for the very next day he recovered to admiration, and was in a short space as well as ever. And yet afterwards, when any would have been speaking of the archprelate (Sharp) in his hearing, he never shewed any resentment, but sometimes would have said somewhat merrily, " Commend him to me for a good physician !"

The last instance I shall give, is in respect of the construction put upon it, as remarkable as any of the former. About the year 1683, Mr Hog, who had some time before that been liberated from the Bass, but on what condition I have not learned,* fell again under the displeasure of the managers ; and being convicted for holding private conventicles, he was banished by the Privy Council, and ordained to remove forth of the kingdom within forty-eight hours, unless he would find caution not to exercise any part of his ministry under a penalty of 5000 merks, over and above performance. This condition he would by no means submit to, and therefore he retired to Berwick within the time limited ; and some time after he went up to London, with a design of transporting himself from thence to Carolina with the first opportunity. But the report of a plot by the Presbyterians against the King and Duke of York having been then industriously propagated by some about the Court, Mr Hog was apprehended as a suspected person, and thrown into prison. After he had lain there a good time, with great patience, his money being near spent, (for be-

* He was confined to Kintyre on the pain of a thousand merks.— Wod. ii. 356.

side his own and servant's maintenance, he paid ten shillings sterling weekly to the keeper for a room, that he might have a place of retirement by himself, and not be put down amongst common felons and ruffians), he says to his servant, "William, I'll set to-morrow apart for prayer, and see that no person be allowed to come in to interrupt me." Accordingly he arose early, and continued close at meditation, prayer, and reading such scriptures as were suggested as matter of argument in prayer, till about twelve o'clock, when a person in the habit of a gentleman desired to speak with him. William Balloch told him his master was retired, and behoved not to be interrupted at that time; but the other interceded that he might tell his master a friend wanted to see him: upon which William, seeing him of a grave and pleasant aspect, reported his desire to his master, who ordered him to shew the gentleman into his chamber. Mr Hog received him courteously, and the other entertained him with a discourse about sufferings for a good God and a good cause, and shewed that "our light afflictions are but for a moment, and not to be compared with the glory that shall be revealed." And having insisted on this subject a few minutes, with great pertinence, power, and spirituality, he arose and embraced Mr Hog most lovingly, exhorted him to a patient continuance in well doing; and then he took out of his pocket a white paper, and gave it to him. Mr Hog finding its weight, understood it was money, and said to the stranger, "Upon what account, Sir, do you give me this money?" The other answered, "Because I am appointed by our great and exalted Master to do so." Mr Hog asked his name, and he refusing to tell, Mr Hog said, "Sir, it is not curiosity that prompts me to ask; but I hope to be enlarged, and then I should account it my duty to call for you at your dwelling in this city, for I suppose you are a citizen of London." The other replied, "You must ask no more questions, but be faithful unto death, and thou shalt have a crown of life;" and then he retired, and Mr Hog never saw him nor heard from him any more "This story I had (says Mr Stuart) from William Balloch, a gracious man, and accounted a person of as great veracity as any of his station in the kingdom, who was an eye and ear witness to what he reported, and said, there was so much majesty and sweetness in the man, and so great an aversion to tell who he was, that he inclined to think he was an angel." But whatever be in that, the interposition of Providence for Mr Hog was extremely seasonable and signal, and he was made to see the Lord humbling himself, and answering his prayer, for when he opened the paper, there was five pounds sterling in it, which to the good man was sweeter than he had got £1000 settled on him yearly, without seeing the glory of infinite wisdom, love, and faithfulness, in the conveyance which shone forth in the gift now made him

Having now seen, that to Mr Hog it was given, on the account of Christ, not only to believe on his name, but also to suffer for his sake, and that the language of the Lord's procedure towards him was like that to the Prophet Daniel, " O man, greatly beloved !" it may be of use for others, that, from Mr James Hog's account of his life, we do shortly represent his principles, with respect to public matters controverted in his day.

Mr Thomas Hog was in his judgment on the side of those called Protesters, and, according to the historians, Messrs Wodrow and Crookshank, he was, in the beginning of the year 1661, deposed by the Synod of Ross, because he would not disclaim that party judicially.

He was clear against hearing the curates, and when questioned for this, he answered, that he looked on himself as obliged by the equity of the thing, and the rather, because of the superadded solemnity of the covenants which he had sworn, to lay out himself in just and regular ways, towards the extirpation of prelacy, with whatsoever belongs to that antichristian hierarchy. And considering the laws enjoined hearing of the curates, as a public test of approbation of, and compliance with His Majesty's ecclesiastic government,

or the supremacy, as explained and declared to be an in-
herent right of the crown, and prelacy, as the king's government ecclesiastic: when he further considered, that all
protestations, remonstrances, and other testimonies against
the same, were by law discharged as seditious, he could see
no other method left of keeping his solemn and sacred oath,
but that of not hearing them; neither could he see that
the patron's presentation, and collation from the bishop, was
the door of access to his ministry, appointed by the Great
Shepherd of the sheep, and therefore could not look upon
a person having these, and no more, as authorized by God,
to carry his message to his people. And, according to Mrs.
Ross, he was the main instrument of licensing the first that
was licensed in Scotland, without compliance of Episcopacy:
and that the first person so licensed was Mr James Fraser
of Brae, we further gather from the original copy of that
gentleman's life, written by himself, chap. ix. sect. 1, though
that whole section, with several other parts of his life, are
omitted in the printed copy.

For the public oaths of that time, Mr Hog was in no
hesitation as to their being established in downright opposition to our vows and covenants, and in several respects
incompatible with Christian liberty and a good conscience.

Touching the indulgences granted by King Charles II,
he agreed with worthy Mr John Brown and Mr Robert
MacWard, and thought honest ministers, as Mr John Welsh,
Mr John Blackader, and others of that sort, were in their
duty, who chose rather to jeopard their lives by preaching
in the fields, than to take shelter under that ensnaring
gourd; yet he upon all occasions expressed a just regard
to the image of Christ wherever he saw it, notwithstanding
of their having different views about matters disputed, and
was utterly against withdrawing from Presbyterian ministers,
who either had not taken the benefit of the indulgence, or,
having taken it, were afterwards ejected, and exposed to
suffering for their integrity; and as he pitied well-meaning
people, who abstained from hearing all except Mr Cameron,

and disapproved what was singular in their opinion; he was at pains to reclaim such of them as he had occasion to see, and prevailed with some, for which others of them were filled with indignation against him, and resented it by names and ways, which some gracious persons amongst them did afterward repent.

Neither could he go all the length that some went in disowning the civil government. That Charles II. and James VII. were our kings, were facts (said he) sadly felt, and what no body could reasonably deny. The Lord in his adorable providence had, for our trial, brought us under these yokes, (as his people of old were captives under the Babylonish Monarch for seventy years), and required us patiently to bear his indignation, until it should please him to open a way for our relief; yet he was of opinion, that in some instances the case was so stated as subjection might be warrantably refused. For instance, in that ticklish case of refusing to pray for the king, wherewith many of the sufferers, towards the end of the persecution, were stigmatized, he could find few, if any, who, when the question was fairly stated, were not disposed, in sincerity, to pray for the king's happiness and salvation, as for their own: but when the barbarous officers, or soldiers, would have required poor labouring men to say off hand, " God save the king," and explained it as meaning in downright terms a praying for God's blessing his Majesty, and prospering him in the (then) present administration of his government, there the ground of suffering was so clearly stated, that several found their hearts filled with joy at being accounted worthy to suffer upon that point alone.

The toleration granted by King James VII. for ushering in his darling popery, in July 1687, was what he did greatly dread, and he did still more detest the flattering and disingenuous addresses sent up to that Prince; yet when he understood that other Presbyterians were improving that liberty with great advantage to their people, and found the infirmities of old age increase upon him, he returned to

Scotland about the beginning of the memorable year 1688, where he staid till the year 1691, at which time his old parishioners finding the way cleared for his reception, sent commissioners to accompany him back to his parish of Kiltearn, where he was received with great joy in June or July that year. But his constitution being broken, he was very unable to discharge his function much in public after that; however, his private conversation became ever the more heavenly, till he entered into the joy of his Lord, the fourth day of January 1692.

King William, of happy memory, having, by the time Mr Hog took possession of his old charge, got leisure to attend to his domestic affairs, and to reward the merit of his friends, resolved on having this good man near him; and for that purpose he sent him a commission to be one of his family chaplains, which was no mean evidence of the sense that penetrating sovereign had of his merit, and of the truth of his prediction concerning himself; but before that honour was bestowed on him, he was seized with the trouble, or rather the complication of troubles, whereof he died.

Amongst the many who visited Mr Hog, " I," says Mr Stuart, "was one. The first time I visited him I preached for him, and the excellency of his conversation (which I shall never forget) engaged me to stay eight days with him. At an after visit, he asked me if I was pre-engaged to settle at Inverness? for I was then a helper there. I told him, I was not to that, nor any place else. ‘Then,’ said he, ‘ have thought of your settlement in this place, for, if I live, I think I will be importuned to go elsewhere ;’ and thereupon he shewed me his patent to be one of King William's chaplains ; ‘and, if I die soon, as I think I shall, in either case, I incline you should succeed me :’ and having told me the disposition of the people, and what qualifications he judged necessary for their edification, he recommended to me to pray upon it, and ask counsel of God concerning it. The greatest length I could, however, go in a matter of that importance while he lived, was to entertain serious thoughts about it; and notwithstanding I found it my duty to conceal the motion, the parishioners were acquainted with his desire, and after his death they were harmonious and zealous in promoting it. In this the desire of his heart was accomplished. It was indeed a great weight on my spirit to succeed so great a man; but I can say, to the praise of sovereign grace, that while I was there, I was powerfully and sweetly supported."

Mr Hog's last sickness was considerably long, and accompanied with great pain. One time, his judicious servant hearing the heavy moans he made, humbly asked him, whether it was soul or bodily pain that extorted such heavy groans from him? To which he replied pleasantly and composedly, "No soul trouble, man, for a hundred and hundred times my Lord hath assured me that I shall be with him for ever; but I am making moan for my body;" and thereupon he entertained him agreeably, concerning the Lord's purging away sin from his own children in this manner, (Isa. xxvii. 9). At another time he said, "Pity me, O ye my friends, and do not pray for my life; you see I have a complication of diseases; allow me to go to my eternal rest;" and then with deep concern of soul he cried, "Look, O my God, upon mine affliction and my pain, and forgive all my sins." And yet, says his servant, never was his conversation more heavenly and spiritual, than when he was thus chastised. Towards his end, he was much feasted with our Saviour's comfortable message to his disciples, (John xx. 17), "I ascend unto my Father and your Father, and to my God and your God." To the writer of the Remarkable Passages he said, " He could not give a look to the Lord, but he was fully persuaded of his everlasting love." And to Mr Stuart he said at another time, "Never did the sun in the firmament shine more brightly to the eyes of my body, than Christ the Sun of Righteousness hath shined on my soul." "Some time after this," continues the same writer, " When I understood that he was very low, I made him my last visit, and when I asked how he did, he answered, 'The unchangeableness of my God is my rock.' Upon Sabbath evening, for I staid with him that week, when I came in from the church, his speech was unintelligible to me, but his servant said he desired me to pray, and commit his soul and body to his God. After prayer I retired a little, and when I returned, I found all present in tears at his dissolution, especially his wife and his faithful servant William Balloch." Mr James Hog and the writer of the Remarkable Passages add, that as Mr Thomas Hog had many times foretold that his Lord and Husband was coming, so in the end he cried out, " Now he is come, he is come, my Lord is come! praises, praises to him for evermore! Amen." And with that word, death closed his eyes.

APPENDIX.

No. I.

CONTAINING·AN ABSTRACT OF MR HOG'S MANNER OF DEALING
WITH PERSONS UNDER CONVICTIONS.

First, he laid down some preliminary observations ; as,

1. That declining or shifting a fair and scriptural inquiry in any concern of religion, is a shrewd sign that matters are utterly wrong, (John iii. 19, 20).

2. That something like a convincing work may have place in some cases, and yet prove delusive, especially, (1.) In the case of melancholy : where this dreadful malady is, it putteth a dismal garb on every thing, and consequently sin must appear terrible also. Evil spirits do ordinarily make a special handle of this disease, to lead to desperate courses. Thus, sin proves in so far a considerable part of the disease. In this case the mind is dark and confused, and according as the malady prevails or abates, the mind is sad or cheerful ; and yet the poor creature can give no reason for either. Besides, melancholy doth ordinarily utterly indispose the patient for action, and rendereth him both unfit and entirely averse from it ; whereas convictions set home upon the conscience by the Spirit of God from the word, are made effectual for exciting to a diligent use of means, as one would do when his house is all in a flame about his ears. Melancholy may be taken off by medicines ; but saving conviction admits of no cure, till the same spirit which awakened, drop in the healing salve as deep as the wound. Yet in the case of several awakened persons, there is a

mixture of this malady; but the Lord overrules it so, as, contrary to its nature, it issues into a distinct concern about their eternal state.   When this is the posture of matters, it is happy if the malady be carried off by medicines, and the soul's concern continue and grow; yet ordinarily in this complex case, the soul's cure bringeth health to the body also, according to Job xxxiii. 23-25, Psal. ciii. 1-3. (2.) Somewhat like to convictions on the mind may be the effect of discontent upon the account of some worldly loss or trouble. ' This is that sorrow which worketh death, (2 Cor. vii. 10).   Such a pretended malady would be cured by bettering the worldly circumstances; yet sometimes this malady hath been blessed of the Lord for ushering in convictions, (2 Chron. xxxiii. 11-13, Job xxxvi. 8, 9, Psal. cvii. 10-13).   And (3.) specious resemblances of soul exercise, are sometimes derived from a secret consciousness of some atrocious and scandalous crime, punishable by the civil powers, or censurable by the church; but here the shame, and not the sin, is that which troubles the soul, (Gen. iv. 13, 14, Matt. xxvii. 3-5).   Yet even such dismal occasions may be made effectual for bringing the soul under a genuine concern about its eternal state; and where that is the case, the patient will be found very willing to glorify God by an open and free acknowledgment, (Psal. li).

3. A third preliminary he laid down was, the detection of the sinner's true estate as a child of the first Adam who had sinned in him, and was now fallen with him, who therefore is in the same state whereinto Satan brought us all by that conquest, and further hardened therein by a course of transgressions.

4. That there is no attaining of any thing that is good and acceptable to the Lord, antecedent to saving faith; or in other words, till we be in Christ. (Heb. xi. 6, Rom. xiv. 23, Matt. vii. 17-19.) And

5. That there is an enlightening work about sin as well as about righteousness carried in upon the conscience by the Spirit of God, in a suitableness to the sinner's circumstantiated case, (John xvi. 8-10).

Secondly, For discovering whether the Holy Spirit was preparing his way towards a saving change on the soul, Mr Hog used to inquire,

1. Where? On what occasion, and from what places of scripture it had pleased the Lord to carry home a conviction of sin upon the conscience? Whether it was particular? Whether the conviction carried from the streams to the fountain of our guilt? And, upon the whole, Whether such a discovery of sin had been diffused through the soul with a strong hand, so as the patient was made to acknowledge his former ignorance of the exceeding sinfulness of his sins, and that he never saw them in the light he now does? (John iv. 29, Rom. iii. 9).

2. Whether the patient had ever found himself under the condemnatory sentence of the broken covenant of works, and so bound justly over to the wrath to come? However various the methods are of the Lord's disposure of his creatures, yet still this holds, that the Spirit of God giveth a true detection of the sinner's state, as it is in reality; for he is the Spirit of truth, and setteth in a true light, what he manifesteth from the word to the conscience, (Heb. iv. 12, Eph. v. 13).

3. He further inquired, How the patient found himself affected with this sentence? This inquiry consisted more especially of two parts, (1.) Whether the weight of this sentence had fallen more heavily upon the conscience, than any worldly loss, pain or trouble, could affect the mind? (Prov. xviii. 14, John vi. 2–4, Acts ii. 37, and xvi. 30, 31.) And (2.) In the event of much felt hardness and confusion, which is usually the case of the patient thus circumstanced, he inquired, Whether this confusion and hardness was looked upon as an evil greater, and to be more lamented, than any worldly loss or trouble? (Isa. i. 6).

Thirdly, For discovering the more rude and unformed beginnings of a gracious and distinguishing change, the heads of inquiry were,

1. Whether in the above case the patient hath had his

mouth stopped in the persuasion of the entire and spotless
equity of the Lord's disposure, being fully convinced that
no person did ever so thoroughly deserve to be cast into
utter darkness? Hence the exercised soul admireth and
adoreth the justice of the judge, and is filled with wonder
at his long suffering patience; and when his proud and daring
spirit putteth forth itself in murmurings, he condemns and
abhors himself for them. These are the gall and wormwood
in his cup, (Judge x. 15).

2. Whether, while the patient is pointing towards the
rich and free mercy of his sovereign Lord, he is troubled
with a two-fold impediment? (1.) A thick and dark vail
of ignorance upon his mind: he knoweth not how to manage,
and is utterly unacquainted with the method of grace, and
he finds that no human instruction can remove this vail,
(Isa. xxv. 7). And (2.) a haughtiness of spirit which hin-
dereth him from submitting to the Lord Jesus Christ, as his
righteousness; and he is made to acknowledge himself as
truly destitute of righteousness, as Christ was entirely free
of sin in his own person, and that of all mankind he stands
most in need of a perfect righteousness.

Fourthly, For discovering the further dawning and nearer
approach of the day of grace, Mr Hog inquired, Whether,
while this matter continued in suspense, the patient found
a firm resolution in the Lord's strength, never to return to
former lords and lovers; and, on the other hand, a firm
resolution, in the same strength, to wait prostrate at the
footstool of sovereign grace, until the day of grace and
mercy break forth, however heavy the delay be? And
where this was the case, it was his opinion, that a gracious
issue was ordinarily near at hand? (Psa. xl. 12, Mic. vii. 7-9,
Psa. xxvii. 14, and lxii. 1, 2).

Fifthly, For discovering the issue of convictions of the
right kind, Mr Hog inquired,

1. Whether (which is chiefly decisive in this matter) the
mind was enlightened to know Christ as he is offered in the
gospel, as our prophet, priest, and king, as made of God

unto us wisdom, righteousness, sanctification, and rede.up-
tion, (1 Cor. i 30). But more especially his character, as
" The Lord our righteousness," (Jer. xxiii. 6), hath its peculiar relation unto the lost, miserable, and undone situation,
wherein the sinner findeth himself at the time? (2 Cor. iv. 6.
Acts xxvi. 18).

2. Whether the soul hath been drawn forth by invincible
power to close with the person of Christ, as standing in a
marriage relation to him, and to receive and rest upon him,
not only as the Saviour in general, but as his Saviour in
particular? according to John 1. xii, Heb. x. 39, Isa.
xxvi. 3, &c.

3. Whether the poor tossed sinner hath found somewhat
of quiet rest in pointing this way under Christ's drawing,
after all his legal resolutions, prayers, fasting, vows, &c., had
utterly failed? (Matt. xi. 28–30, Luke xv. 16–18, Psa.
lxxxix. 19, Jer. xvii. 5, 6, Acts iv. 12, Heb. iv. 3).

4. Whether, according to the measure of the knowledge
that the person hath got of the glory of God in the face of
Jesus Christ, a pleasant sense of gratitude, and impression
of the love of Christ, have strongly and sweetly engaged the
soul to the whole of new obedience, without exception or
reserve? (Ps. xviii. 1. and cxvi. 1, 2 Cor. v. 14). And,

5. Whether under all subsequent burden by sin, of whatsoever sort, or by the fruits of the same, the main propen-
sity of the soul be to seek ease and relief in the humble
acknowledgment of guilt before the Lord, and by faith im-
ploring pity and pardon for Christ's sake alone? (Psa. xxxii.
2–5, Prov. xxviii. 13, 1 John i .9, Hos. v. 15, Lev. xxvi.
40–42).

But, upon the whole, it was Mr Hog's opinion, that in
judging of soul-exercise, we should have a special respect to
the issues, for that it is very difficult, if at all possible,
before the respective issues, to fix the difference betwixt
what is right and kindly, and that which may issue in a
further strengthening of Satan's kingdom, (Luke xi. 24 .26)
Much depends upon the cool, or cure, of these soul fevers,

which will prove either health or ruin to the patient, if sovereign and free mercy set not matters right again, (John xvi. 8, 9.) Conviction of sin is best verified by the subsequent conviction of righteousness, and that again by conviction of judgment.

No. II.

ACCOUNT OF MR THOMAS HOG OF KILTEARN, EXTRACTED FROM MS. MEMOIRS OF JAMES NIMMO, COUNCILLOR AND TREASURER OF EDINBURGH. *Wodrow MS.*

" How pleasant did the Lord at length make the godly in that place* to me, and particularly that singularly holy man of God, Mr Thomas Hog, who was a true father to our Israel, and to whom all that feared the Lord, that knew him, had a great deference, yea, enemies themselves, he being not only endued with much of the mind of God, but also with much of a clear judgment and a solid sound mind; and albeit courteous to all, yet would not omit with authority to reprove sin in any, but still with such gaining wisdom, that all feared him, the godly loved him, and enemies could find nothing against him except in the matters of his God, when he would not yield a hoof; and yet managed with that respect and discretion towards enemies, that often they were made to admire him; for in his Master's concerns he spoke as one having authority, yet without the least evidence of rancour or irritation always. In his younger years he, and that eminently pious woman Mrs Ross by her husband, and Katherine Collace by name, by providence were made acquaint, and both being deeply exercised in soul, by the blessing of the Lord were helped to build up one another in Christ Jesus. And thereby the Lord made them signally useful to others in like cases, and particularly

* Murray or Nairnshire.

Mr Hog, whom the Lord called forth more remarkably in his particular calling: who albeit the Lord gave him no children, yet the Lord once gave him powerfully that scripture, and fulfilled it to him, " I will give thee a name better than of sons and daughters," making him the instrument of begetting many sons and daughters to the Lord. And it was his great care, as a father, to convince and humble them by the Lord's assistance, and then to comfort and confirm them in due time; to do which the Lord, both by preaching and conference, singularly assisted him, more I judge than any in his day." He "had come from the south, where he had been prisoner long for his faithfulness, and at once eighteen months in the castle of the Bass." P. 37–39.

" Some time before," January 29th 1682, he, " after long imprisonment, was come north, under bond given for his friends, to answer the king's council when called." P. 29.

" About the beginning of March 1683, Mr Hog had sent his godly servant, William Balloch, to warn Nimmo, that at a ball in Kilravoch, Lord Doune, (son of the Earl of Moray,) swore if he was in Murray he would have Nimmo laid in prison, who thereupon went south to Edinburgh, and thence to Berwick." P. 67, 75.

Here, on its environs, they continued to reside, when on " the first of November [1683] our dear and worthy friend, Mr Thomas Hog, who was out of prison upon bond to answer the council at call, was then to appear before them," p. 86. " Our dear and worthy friend, Mr Hog, was banished by act of council to be out of the kingdom of Scotland in forty-eight hours' time under severe penalties. They indeed offered him six weeks to provide for his banishment, if he would give bond, as some had done, not to exercise any part of his ministerial function during that time. He told them, it was like, being under much frailness of body, he would not be able; but as he had his commission from God, he would not bind up himself one hour, if the Lord called him and gave him strength: and therefore so little time was allowed. So he caused a coach, agreed for, to come to the tolbooth door and take him in ; and upon April 3, he came to Berwick, to the great comfort of our minds," " My wife's intimate friend, Mrs Hog, also several others of some note of our own land." P. 88, 89.

Nimmo and Hog had their houses near to each other, and "one day there came certain word of a general search through the town ; and accordingly, after dinner the garrison began, and the ports were closed, and houses searched, and haylofts, the hay overturned with great pains. They began at the next house where Mr Hog and I went, and searched round, and so our house was last, and a mercy also. Mr Hog went to a private closet behind the hinging (bed-curtain), and I went up to a little place for doves, above a fore stair, where I could only sit or lie, but not stand, to which only a deal (deal-board) did lift and came down again, so exactly as made of purpose ; and so we were in prisons till they went the round of search ; and against they came back to our house it was growing dark, and they much fatigued, and   *   *   *   our landlord, a true friend, met them at the entry, and said he judged they were weary ; would they take a bottle of his ale and beer ? to which they willingly agreed and accepted of. And he did carry pleasantly, and diverted them for some time, and told them, an old woman his mother lived in the lodging beside him, and if they pleased they might go in and see there was none else there ; which they refused, saying they would not trouble the old gentlewoman, and so were gone. And immediately the landlord came to Mr Hog and me, and took us in his arms, with as much joy as if he had got a prize, said that all was over, and so we mercifully escaped them." P 95, 96.

Kennoway having said, if Nimmo was out of hell he would have him, (at hearing of which, blessed Mr Hog said, " If ye were in heaven, I fear he would not win there to seek you,") p. 110, 111, " I resolved, if the Lord would, to go abroad. And Mr Hog being to go for London, to see if there was any encouragement to go to Carolina, and thereby my faithful companion in tribulation, my wife, was to be left alone in a garrisoned town. About the 8th of April (1685), I was resolving to go to London with Mr Hog. The day before we were to go, Mr Hog asked me, if the Lord had given me full clearance to go. I told him I had some peace, but not that desired clearance. He desired me to take some time apart to seek the Lord's mind on that matter, and said, "Albeit you would be desirable to me, yet I advise either to get full clearance, or not to go." Nimmo took time, and "resolved to stay, and had peace therein, but it displeased Mrs Hog; but her husband sweetly complied, and he and his godly servant went." In a little time after Mr Hog went, there was a great report of an invasion both to Scotland and England; and shortly after Mr Hog came to London, he was jealoused (suspected) for a spy and trafficker for Monmouth, taken, and the English oaths offered; and upon refusing to take them, both he and servant were sent to prison." P. 115–117.

Before shipping at Burntisland, on 23d November 1685, "we heard some report that Mr Hog was liberated at London, and gone for Holland, which was ground of encouragement." "Before we came from Scotland, there had come a line from Mr Hog, giving account of his being safe at Rotterdam, to whom, when landed, (4th December 1685,) we went and staid with him some few nights, till we got the foresaid chamber; and, indeed, he and his wife were our parents to their power." P. 127, 128.

20th October 1686, Nimmo having domestic anxieties, observes, "Our blest father and friend, Mr Hog, was gone the term of Whitsunday before to the Hague, where I some time went, and as his company and advice were refreshing, so my going there was refreshing. Some time after, (after the 5th of November,) as he had baptized our eldest son John, so we took this second to the Hague to him, where he was baptized James; at which time was such signal and observable power and presence of the Lord, that not only I but others were made to say, they never heard nor felt more of the authority of the Lord in any ordinance, than when he pronounced his name, and the names of the persons of the ever blessed Trinity." P. 133, 134.

" Even in this place, the fugitives in Rotterdam were not without danger from the enemy; for some were without order gripped, put aboard, and sent for England, and there hanged, some alleged murdered : in that place where we were, some, attacked by violence with sword in hand, to be carried off, and they defending themselves, resisting force with force, in wounds and blood, till the magistrates of Rotterdam took and imprisoned both till examined, and by the mob forced to justice, albeit inclinable enough to themselves; and some of these attackers were in prison when the Prince of Orange came over at the happy revolution. And sometimes there was a search procured by King James from the States; but they kindly gave some advertisement, that Scots people might be on their guard; as particularly one for Sir James Stewart, who narrowly escaped by the importunity of old Mr Hog, in whose house he was, that he would go out, having heard the search (which put us all in alarm) was to be that night." P. 135.

On King James' toleration, " severals went home. Albeit our worthy friend Mr Hog never joined therewith, so as to preach by virtue thereof, yet, after seeking the Lord, he determined and went to Scotland, which was a great seeming loss to me." P. 136.

Mrs Hog came home with Nimmo to Edinburgh on the 1st of May 1688. Mr Hog gave Nimmo his advice in his household affairs. About January 1690, Nimmo's third son was born, and named Thomas, " after blessed Mr Hog, who had married us, and baptized our three former children in three several nations." P. 148, 138, 139, 145.

No. III.

MR HOG'S DEPOSITION.

So well was the deprecated act (which overturned Presbyterianism and set up Episcopacy in its place) received by the time-serving Synod of Ross, that they urged it into effect against one of their own body, more than a year before the ejection of the other non-conforming clergymen. In a meeting of the Synod which took place in 1661, the person chosen as moderator was one Murdoch Mackenzie; —a man so strong in his attachments, that he had previously sworn to the National Covenant no fewer than fourteen times, and he had now fallen as desperately in love with the Bishoprick of Moray. One of his brethren, however, an unmanageable, dangerous person, for he was uncompromisingly honest, and possessed of very considerable talent, stood directly in the way of his preferment. This member, the celebrated Mr Hog of Kiltearn, had not sworn to the Covenant half so often as his superior, the Moderator, but then so wrong-headed was he as to regard his few oaths as binding; and he could not bring himself to like Prelacy any the better for its being espoused by the king. And so his expulsion was evidently a matter of necessity. The Moderator had nothing to urge against his practice: for no one could excel him in the art of living well; but his opinions lay more within his reach; and no sooner had the Synod met, than singling him out, he demanded what his thoughts were of the Protesters—the party of Presbyterians who, about ten years before, had not taken part with the king against the Republicans. Mr Hog declined to answer; and on being removed, that the Synod might deliberate, the Moderator rose and addressed them. Their brother of Kiltearn, he said, was certainly a great man—a very great man, but as certainly were the Protesters opposed to the king; and if any member of Synod took part with them, whatever his character, it was evidently the duty of the other members to have him expelled. Mr Hog was then called in, and having refused, as was anticipated, judicially to disown the Protesters, sentence of deposition was passed against him. But the consciences of the men who thus dealt with him, betrayed in a very remarkable manner their real estimate of his conduct. It is stated by Wodrow, on the authority of an eye-witness, that sentence was passed with a peculiar air of veneration, as if they were ordaining him to some higher office; and that the Moderator was so deprived of his self-possession as to remind him, in a consolatory speech, that " our Lord Jesus Christ had suffered great wrong from the Scribes and Pharisees."—(*From Miller's Scenes and Legends of the North of Scotland.*)

No. IV.

TRADITIONARY NOTICES OF MR THOMAS HOG.

While this portion of the Work was going through the press, the following notices of Hog were kindly transmitted by the Rev. William Barclay, minister of the Free Church, Arr, Nairn, which we consider too interesting to be omitted :—

" The tradition is still preserved here, and I never heard a doubt of the fact expressed, that Mr Thomas Hog settled for some time at Knockowdie, in this parish (of Auldearn) which is doubtless the same as what is called *Knockgaudy*, in the memoir to which you refer. The tradition also is, that he preached the gospel not only in his private house there, but also in other places in the neighbourhood. His principal preaching station was on the farm of Dalmore, belonging to the curate of Lethen, on which farm our Free Church is built; and there is a deep valley on that farm, through which a small stream flows, that is generally dried up in summer, but which is pretty large in times of rain, in which valley he was wont to assemble his congregation, and in which he dispensed to them the sacrament of the Lord's Supper. The place is called Hog's Stripe to this day; and the stone on which he sat during the time the congregation was singing is still there. The place is very near to Knockowdie. Between these two places there flows a stream, called there *the burn of Dalmore,*—and below that, *the burn of Auldearn,* over which there was a bridge, which was called *the clattering brig.* It was a very low bridge, and rude in its construction, being formed by laying a flag or two upon some stones rudely built up at each side; and the tradition says, that on one occasion, when Mr Hog was pursued by his persecutors, he hid himself under that bridge, and that while he was hid there, he heard his persecutors pass over it, swearing, that if he was on this side of hell, they would find him. The tradition also says, that he was in the way of preaching at Lethen; and that on one occasion, when he was preaching there, he observed a man laugh at something which he had said; upon which Mr Hog paused, and desired his congregation to mark that man, and see whether some signal token of the divine displeasure would not soon overtake him; and before the next morning the man was dead. This is the substance of the tradition which exists in this neighbourhood on the subject. The success with which God blessed his ministry is also spoken of."

AN

ABBREVIATE OF THE LIFE

OF THE

REV. MR HENRY ERSKINE,

MINISTER OF THE GOSPEL.

BY HIS SON.

WITH SOME ADDITIONS BY MR WILLIAM VEITCH.

AN ABBREVIATE OF THE LIFE

OF THE

REV. HENRY ERSKINE.

MR HENRY ERSKINE was born in the year 1624, in a village called Dryburgh, the seat of an ancient abbacy in the Merse, upon the river Tweed, in the kingdom of Scotland. His father, Ralph Erskine of Shielfield, was a gentleman of a competent fortune, whose posterity still have their ordinary residence in Dryburgh, being descended of the ancient family of Mar.* Ralph Erskine had about thirty-

---

* The Erskines of Shielfield are the descendants of David Erskine, commendator of Dryburgh, a natural son of Robert, Master of Erskine, who was eldest son of John, the fifth Earl of Mar, of the name of Erskine, and of Lady Margaret Campbell, eldest daughter of Archibald, second Earl of Argyle. Robert was also nephew of John Earl of Mar, who was chosen Regent of Scotland in the year 1571. He was killed at the battle of Pinkie, on the 10th of September 1547, without legitimate issue. Different accounts have been given of the origin of the name. Some think it is derived from the lands of the barony called the Barony of Erskine, on the Clyde, the property of the family of Mar for many ages. Others give the following account of its origin : " In the reign of Malcolm II. a Scotchman having killed with his own hand Enric, a Danish general, at the battle of Murthill, cut off his head, and with the bloody dagger in his hand shewed it to the king, in the Gaelic *Eris Skyne*, alluding to the head and dagger, and in the same language also said, 'I intend to perform greater actions than what I have done,' whereupon Malcolm imposed on him the sirname of Erskine, [*i. e.* the man with the dagger,] and assigned for his armorial bearing a hand holding a dagger, with *Je pense plus*, for a motto ; still the crest and motto of the noble family of Mar." (Douglas' Peerage of Scotland, vol. ii. p. 206, 211.)

three children, his son Henry being among the youngest.
After he (Henry) had finished his course of philosophy at
Edinburgh, he applied himself to the study of divinity; and
the ministers being pleased with his proficiency, both in the
speculative and practical part thereof, he was first licensed
to preach, and afterwards was ordained minister of Cornhill (in Durham), about ten miles distant from Dryburgh,
on the English side. He continued only about three years*
minister in this place, before he was ejected by the Act of
Uniformity.†

When he came first to be minister at Cornhill, the people
were so rude and barbarous, that he could have heard them,
when sitting in his own house, cursing him in the open
streets. However, through the blessing of God on his labours, a remarkable change was wrought in them before he
left the place, insomuch, that with the Galatians, many of
them would, if possible, have plucked out their eyes and
given them to him, for his Master's sake. An evidence of
this you will see in the following passage. Immediately
after his ejection, and before the place was filled up by the
bishop, some honest people in the congregation advised Mr
Erskine to labour the glebe, which accordingly was at-
tempted; but was immediately stopped by the agents of
the Bishop, who employed some to labour it for his use
While the workmen are tilling, one of them begins to regret
it to his neighbour as a hardship, that Mr Erskine should

* The precise duration of his ministry at Cornhill seems to be in-
volved in some degree of uncertainty. Palmer and Calamy make it as
here only three years. (Palmer's Nonconformist's Memorial, vol. iii.
p. 62. Calamy's Continuation, vol. ii. p. 678). Palmer says, "Cornhill
chapel, in the parish of Norham." Randall has it, "A Scot, an intruder,
1649." Wodrow says, that he was ordained minister at Cornhill about
the year 1649, (History of the Sufferings of the Church of Scotland, vol.
iii. p. 403); and, according to this account, he must have been minister
of that place thirteen years.

† The sweeping Act of Uniformity, commonly called the Bartholomew
Act, by which in one day, on the 24th of August 1662, about 2000 of
the best ministers of the English Church were ejected from their
charges, for Nonconformity.

I

be deprived of the glebe, especially, when there was no other incumbent. His neighbour to whom he spoke, answered in a rude and disdainful manner, " Tush ! I don't value who have it; before I eat, or ——*, or ——*, I'll do my darg." But before the plough had gone twice or thrice about the land, the person who thus expressed himself was seized with an iliac passion, of which he died in a day or two, so that he never did any of the three. The hand of God was so visible in this providence, and struck the inhabitants of the place with such consternation and fear, that not one would be prevailed with to put a plough in the ground that year for the bishop's behoof, so that Mr Erskine's friends had liberty to plough it, to sow and reap it for his use; and it was observable, that the glebe that year yielded an excellent crop, which served Mr Erskine's family of bread for a long time after.

During his incumbency in Cornhill he received no stipend, and therefore was advised, after his ejection, to repair to London, and petition his majesty for a warrant to uplift it.

Accordingly, he undertakes the journey by sea; but Providence so ordered it, that the ship in which he was passenger was forced into Harwich harbour, where she lay wind-bound for the space of three weeks. The people there understanding him to be an outed minister, were desirous he should preach the gospel among them during his continuance in that place, which accordingly he did every Sabbath, and sometimes also upon the week days, for which they gave him a very handsome compliment when he went off. Being arrived at London, he presented his petition to his Majesty King Charles, to the effect foresaid; but though he made what interest he could, and waited for an answer till any money he had brought with him was near spent, he was at length sent off with this answer, that no stipend could be had, unless he conformed to the worship of the Established Church. Some considerable benefices were

* Here an omission is purposely made, the words that follow being too coarse for insertion.

offered him by some Scots nobility of his acquaintance at court, providing he would conform; but he rejected all proposals of this nature, declaring that he would rather venture himself and his family on the care of Providence, though he and they should beg their bread, than run cross to the light of his conscience.

Finding that nothing was to be done about court, he agrees with a ship-master designed for Leith, to bring him to Scotland. Some while after they had launched, Mr Erskine needing a refreshment, calls for a ship-boy to change him a crown, which was all the superplus of his expenses at London. The boy, after he had looked to it, told him his crown was not worth a farthing. Upon this, he addresses himself to the master of the ship, communicates his strait to him, telling him that he hoped to be supplied by friends at Edinburgh, if it should please God to send them safely there. But Providence saw to his supply before he came that length; for after they were some leagues past Harwich, the wind turns, a terrible storm arises, whereby they were driven they scarce knew whither. Sometimes he heard the mariners crying, " Steer for the coast of Norway !" sometimes, " Steer for the coast of Holland !" However, He whom the seas and winds obey so ordered it, that they were at length forced into Harwich, among Mr Erskine's friends, the haven he much desired; and for the space of six weeks the wind blew full in the mouth of that harbour, so that they could not stir out of the place all that time. During this interval, Mr Erskine preached every Sabbath, and frequently also through the week, for which they rewarded him liberally when he went off. When he began to relate to his fellow-passengers what had been his strait, and how he was supplied, what kindness he had met with in the place, and what service he had been doing his Master, they were all convinced that he was the Jonah for whose sake the storm had been raised, and that they had been detained prisoners in Harwich upon his account, for such a long time. The master of the ship, after they were

come to Leith, was so kind, that he would have nothing of
him, either for his freight or maintenance.

The people of Harwich conceived such a liking to him
during his abode in the place, that they were very earnest
he would return, and bring his wife and family along with
him, promising him suitable encouragement.   He himself
was very much inclined to gratify their desire, but his wife
would by no means condescend to go so far abroad from
her friends and country.

Being returned to Cornhill, he transported himself and
his family to Dryburgh, the place of his nativity, where he
had a house from his elder brother, John Erskine of Shielfield.   Here he continued preaching, sometimes in his own
house, and sometimes in the open field as occasion offered,
until he was forced to leave the kingdom ; the occasion of
which was as follows :—

In the year 1682, April the 23d, the laird of Meldrum*
came upon him with a company of soldiers, while he was
worshipping God in his family, it being the Lord's day,
and carried him away to Melrose, two miles from Dryburgh;
and on the morrow a 5000 merk bond was given in for his
appearance when called, James Erskine of Shielfield, Mr
Erskine's nephew, being bondsman.

Meldrum, upon the 8th of May following, being come
back to Melrose from the west of Scotland, calls for Mr
Erskine and his bondsman, and having given up the bond,
carries Mr Erskine to Jedburgh, where again he found bail
for his appearance before him at Edinburgh the 12th of
May.   The ague had seized Mr Erskine in a violent manner ; yet he was obliged to wait on at the time appointed ;†

* Adam Urquhart, a very active instrument in persecuting the Presbyterians, as we learn from Wodrow's History.

† Fraser informs us, that "one of Mr Erskine's descendants is possessed of an ebony cabinet, formerly the property of Mr Ralph Erskine
of Dunfermline, containing a number of small family relics, including
a pair of *thummikins*, with which, according to tradition, the good man
had the honour of being invested at the time he was taken prisoner to
Edinburgh."—(Memoir of Rev. Henry Erskine, prefixed to the Life of
Ebenezer Erskine, p. 16.)

and being brought before a Committee of the Privy Council, Sir George M'Kenzie, the king's advocate, asked him, if he would give bond to preach no more at conventicles; which Mr Erskine refused, saying, "I have my commission from Christ, and though I were within an hour of my death, I durst not lay it down at any mortal man's feet." The advocate having reported this to the Council, his affair was delayed till the 6th of June following, having found bail for his compearance at that time, under the pain of 4000 merks.

Upon the 6th of June he was convened before the Council, and a libel being read (which, with the summons, had been sent him on June the 2d), charging him for preaching at conventicles, disorderly baptizing, and marrying; Chancellor Haddon Gordon asked him, what he had to say to the libel? He answered, that he denied the whole, adding, that it was well known to all who lived about him, that from September the 22d, anno [16]81, to the end of February [16]82, the Lord's hand was upon him by a white flux, so sore, that he was not in a case to bow a knee before God in his family, or so much as to crave God's blessing on his meat; and that after February, he had been seized by a violent ague, which laid him under an incapacity of performing his ministerial work. The Chancellor asked him, if he would depone that he had not preached, baptized, or married, from September to June? Answered, that he was not free to give his oath for the whole of that time.

Nota.—This was a procedure quite cross to the maxim received and asserted by Sir George M'Kenzie in his book of Criminals, where he owns, that in criminal cases (as this was by the laws of Scotland then in being) "*Nemo tenetur jurare in sui injuriam,*" (no one is bound to give oath to what will injure himself).

However, though nothing was proven against him, he was immediately sentenced to pay 5000 merks of fine, to go to the tolbooth of Edinburgh that night, and from thence to be carried to the Bass to-morrow, and to lie there till the fine was paid, and bond given that he should preach no more.

To prevent, if possible, his going to the Bass, he gave in a petition that afternoon to the Council, desiring that the sentence might be changed, and liberty granted to go off the nation, promising to find caution for his so doing. Through the interest of friends this favour was granted, and accordingly, upon the 14th of June, Mr Erskine's nephew, John Brown of Park (living at present) bound himself in a bond of 5000 merks, that Mr Erskine, within fourteen days, should remove out of the kingdom, never to return without liberty granted; and that same day he was let out of the prison, the clerks of the Council having got one-and-twenty dollars, and the jailor with his servants, four.*

Having provided himself for his journey, taken farewell of his friends, of his wife, and children, he removed out of the kingdom within the time prefixed, not knowing of any certain abode. He went first to the county of Northumberland on the English side; but not finding it safe for him to stay there, he went to the county of Cumberland, and at last fixed in a place called Parkridge, about ten miles

* In Chambers' General Biographical Dictionary, it is stated, that "the persecution carried on at that time in Scotland against the Presbyterians, obliged Mr Erskine to take refuge in Holland, whence want of the common necessaries of life induced him again to return to his native country, where he was apprehended and committed prisoner to the Bass, a strong fort in the mouth of the Forth. There he continued near three years, till, through the interest of the then Earl of Mar, his kinsman, he was set at liberty; but such was the violence of the times, that he was again driven from Scotland." There is, however, no evidence that Mr Erskine ever went to Holland, nor that he was ever a prisoner in the Bass. Had these statements been matter of fact, it is not very probable that either of them, and particularly the last, would have been omitted in this Abbreviate of his Life by his Son. In the same Biographical Work it is affirmed, that Ebenezer Erskine was born in the prison of the Bass; a statement which must be unfounded. We have not only no evidence that either of his parents was ever imprisoned in the Bass, but we know that at the time of his birth, June 22d, 1680, his parents were residing at Dryburgh, in a great measure free from molestation;—this was two years before he was apprehended by Urquhart of Meldrum, and sentenced to be imprisoned in the Bass.

distance from Carlisle, the proprietor of the place having offered him a dwelling-house. Thither he sent for his wife and small children, September the 22d, and there they lived for about the space of two years,* until he was invited by one Mr Philip Gray of Preston, to live under him, in an obscure place, called Monilaws, about a mile's distance from Cornhill, where he had formerly been minister. This kind offer of Mr Gray's he accepted, and accordingly transported himself and his family thither,† but was not in safety there either; for July the 2d, [16] 85, he was apprehended by eight of the militia horsemen, and carried to Wooler; on the morrow to Fowberrie, to Colonel Struthers, who told him that he must go to Newcastle to Sir John Fenwick, by virtue of an order from the king; and that night was sent back to Wooler prison, where he met with Mr Ogle,‡

* It is not unlikely that it was while residing at Parkridge, that the following instance of the success of his ministry took place; which we shall give in the words of the Rev. John Brown, Whitburn. "While living in an obscure place at Mossbank, on the English border, he enjoyed eminent success in preaching a sermon. As he was walking one day for his recreation, he observed several young people—who had been digging peats—during the time they were allowed to rest, diverting themselves. In his grave manner he says, 'I think you are too merry.' To which one of them replied, 'We suppose you are a minister; if you preach a sermon to us, we will sit down and be grave.' 'I fear you are not,' said Mr Erskine, 'in a proper frame for hearing a sermon.' They, however, pressed him so much, that at last he yielded. After retiring a little into a secret place for prayer, he came, and preached to about thirty persons. This issued in the conversion of eleven of them to the faith of the gospel."—(Memorials of the Nonconformist Ministers, p. 72).

† It was at Monilaws that his son Ralph, who became minister of Dunfermline, and one of the Fathers of the Secession, was born, March 15, 1685, old style.

‡ Mr Luke Ogle was minister for some time at Inghram; and was afterwards removed to Berwick-upon-Tweed. On account of his opposition to Prelacy, like many others, he was ejected in 1662. Some time after his ejection, he went to London to complain of several instances of cruel treatment which he met with, to General Monk, who when residing in Berwick had shewed him much kindness and respect, and by whom he therefore expected to be befriended. The General received him in the most courteous manner, and told him that provided he

his fellow-prisoner.   Saturday, July the 4th, Mr Ogle and he were carried away to Eglingham, to the Justice-house, guarded with nine troopers.   There they tarried till Monday, at which time, Mr Erskine was seized with a violent colic, of which he thought to have died ; yet such was the barbarity of the soldiers, that away he must go in the greatest extremity of torment, every moment expecting to have fallen down from his horse; though it pleased God he was carried through.   About seven at night they arrived at Newcastle, at Sir John Fenwick's gate, who forthwith ordered them to prison.   Not being satisfied with imprisoning their persons, they took their horse from them by violence.

Mr Erskine's sickness and pain still continuing, the prisoners dealt with the jailor on his behalf, that he might have liberty to go out of prison for a time, which was obtained ; and after his recovery, he returned to prison.   His landlady, Mrs Man, though none of his acquaintance, would have nothing for his entertainment during his fourteen days' sickness.

Upon the 22d of the same month of July, Mr Ogle and he were liberate (upon the Act of Indemnity), and at his

would conform, he would use his influence to obtain a Bishoprick for him ; but that otherwise, he could do him no service.   Mr Ogle declined the offer, and humbly and meekly expressed.it to be his highest ambition to live peaceably among his people, and that if this was not granted him, he behoved to submit to the will of Providence.   For some years he preached privately at Bowden, where he had a small. estate; not, however, without being subjected to molestation.   After the Indulgence granted by King James. an invitation being given him, he returned to Berwick, and collected a numerous congregation. While here, he was called to Kelso, and afterwards to Edinburgh; but nothing could induce him to leave Berwick, where God had so signally blessed his labours.   He continued there till his death, which took place in the sixty-seventh year of his age, April 1696; only a few months before the death of his friend and fellow-sufferer, Mr Erskine.   Dr Calamy describes him as " a man of great learning, and particularly well skilled in ecclesiastical history."—(Calamy's Continuation, vol. ii. pp. 500-503).

departure, the prisoners were so kind, that they gave him thirty shillings sterling, to carry his charges home.

He continued at Monilaws, preaching the gospel for ordinary every Lord's day, until the year 1687, at which time King James's toleration being granted, a body of people of the Presbyterian persuasion in the parish of Whitsom, and places adjacent on the Scots side, gave him a call to be their minister ; which he accepted ; they having got up his bond (already mentioned) from the Council of Scotland, which his son Ebenezer has lying by him, as an authentic document of the story.

His family removed from Monilaws in England, to Revelaw in Scotland, in the parish of Whitsom, September the 1st, 1687, where he preached in a meeting-house till the happy Revolution,* at which time he was called to be

* One instance of the success of his ministry at Whitsom is eminently worthy of being recorded, and held in grateful remembrance—the conversion of Thomas Boston, the well-known author of " Man's Fourfold State." To the period when this gracious change was wrought upon his heart, Boston often looked back in after life ; and while he traced the change to the free and unmerited grace of God, he felt the affection of a son towards the instrument of his conversion. He thus speaks of it in his Memoirs.—(Pp. 8, 9, 10.)

"During the first years of my being at the grammar school, I kept the kirk punctually, where I heard those of the Episcopal way ; that being then the national Establishment : but I knew nothing of the matter, save to give suit and presence within the walls of the house ; living without God in the world, unconcerned about the state of my soul, till the year 1687. Toward the latter end of summer that year, the liberty of conscience being then newly given by King James, my father took me away with him to a Presbyterian meeting, in the Newton of Whitsom. There I heard the worthy Mr Henry Erskine, minister of Cornhill before the Restoration, by whose means it pleased the Lord to awaken me, and bring me under exercise about my soul's state ; being then going in the twelfth year of my age. * * * * Two of Mr Erskine's first texts were, " Behold the Lamb of God," &c. (John i. 29) ; and, " O generation of vipers, who hath warned you to flee ?" &c. (Matt. iii. 7). I distinctly remember that from this last, he ofttimes forewarned of judgments to come on these nations, which I still apprehend will come. By these I judge God spake to me ; however, I know I was touched quickly after the first hearing, wherein I was like one amazed with some new and strange thing. My lost state by nature and minister of Chirnside, the Presbytery seat of that bounds, about five miles' distance from Berwick; and there he continued minister till the day of his death, August the 10th, 1696, the seventy-second year of his age.

It were an injury done to good Providence, and to the memory of this worthy person, to conceal some other memorable appearances of Providence for his supply in the midst of these hardships which he suffered from the hand of man. I shall condescend upon two or three, which I had from his own mouth, when living, and which he told to many yet alive in Scotland and England. When he dwelt at Dryburgh, after his ejection from Cornhill, having no visible way of living, he and his family were reduced several times to great straits. However, their extremity was ordinarily God's opportunity of providing for them; so that neither he nor his were ever put to beg their bread.

But to come to particulars: Upon a certain time, the barrel of meal and cruse of oil were entirely spent; so that after the family had supped at night, there remained neither bread, meal, flesh, nor money in the house. They go to

my absolute need of Christ, being thus discovered to me, I was set to pray in earnest; but remember, nothing of that kind I did before, save what was done at meals, and in my bed. I also carefully attended for ordinary the preaching of the word at Rivelaw, where Mr Erskine had his meeting-house, near about four miles from Dunse. In the summer time, company could hardly be missed; and with them something to be heard, especially in the returning, that was for edification, to which I listened; but in the winter, sometimes it was my lot to go alone, without so much as the benefit of a horse to carry me through Blackadder Water, the wading whereof in sharp frosty weather, I very well remember. But such things were then easy, for the benefit of the word, which came with power." In some of his other writings he refers to the same subject. In his *Soliloquy on the Art of Man-fishing*, he thus addresses his soul,— "Little wast thou thinking, O my soul, on Christ, heaven, or thyself, when thou went to the Newton of Whitsom to hear a preaching, when Christ first dealt with thee, where thou got an unexpected cast!" And again he says to his soul, "Consider what a sad case thou thyself wast in when Christ concerned himself for thy good. Thou wast going on in the way to hell, as blind as a mole: at last, Christ opened thine eyes, and let thee see thy hazard, by a preacher that was none of the unconcerned Gallios; who spared neither his body, his credit, nor reputation to gain thee and the like of thee."

rest; but no sooner is the morning dawned, but the little children begin to call for their "morning piece," as we call it in Scotland. Mr Erskine being of a cheerful temper under all vicissitudes of Providence, bids them arise and dance, and he would play them a spring upon the citer (cittern or guitar) till their breakfast should be ready for them. However, while he is thus diverting the children, and encouraging himself and his wife to depend upon Providence, which feeds the young ravens when they cry to God for food, they hear horse-feet coming along the house side, and within a little, a rude fellow raps hard at the door, calling for some to help him off with his load. Being asked whence he came, and whither he was going, he told that the Lady Reburn had sent him with what he had on horseback, to Mr Erskine. They told him, that surely he was in a mistake, and that probably he was sent to —— Erskine of Shielfield, in the same town. "No," says he, "I'm not such a sot as you take me to be,—it's to Mr Henry Erskine; come, help off with the load, otherwise I'll throw it down at the door." The sack being carried in and opened, they found it well packed both with flesh and meal in abundance for the present necessity : which providence encouraged him to depend on his bountiful Benefactor in future straits of the same nature.

At another time, being in Edinburgh, he was reduced to such a strait for want of money, that having only two or three halfpennies in his pocket, he was ashamed to go in to any public inn, to call for victuals, lest his stock had not answered the reckoning; therefore he resolved to take a turn upon the street, till dinner time should be over. While he is laying down this resolution with himself, there comes a person to him in a countryman's habit, asking if his name was Master Henry Erskine? to which he answered in the affirmative, asking what his business was with him? "I have," replied he, "a letter for you;" which accordingly he delivers, and in the letter were inclosed seven Scots ducatoons, nothing being written in the letter but these words,

" Sir, Receive this from a sympathising friend. Farewell,"
without any subscription. Mr Erskine being desirous to
know his kind benefactor, invites the honest man to go in to
a house hard by, and take a drink with him. Having got
him alone, he begins to interrogate him, who sent him? The
honest man told him that he was enjoined secrecy, therefore
must be excused as to that matter, for he could not betray
his trust. However, Mr Erskine still insisted, asking a
great many questions, that at least he may know what
airth of the world he had come from. The man finding
him somewhat inquisitive, desires him to sit a little till he
went forth; but being once gone, he never returned, neither
did Mr Erskine ever come to know his benefactor.

Being at another time called to undertake a journey on
foot, when he had nothing to bear his charges while he is
upon his way, nature obliges him to step aside towards a
bush of rushes. There, being about to fix the end of his
staff in the marsh ground, the end of it tinkles upon a sum
of money, being two half-crowns, which were very steadable
to him all the time, and carried his charges home.

He was an able and faithful minister of the New Testament;
he preached the gospel in season and out of season, and many
times with the peril of his life. He commonly delivered
his Master's message with a peculiar vivacity and liveliness,
and had the seal of his ministry upon many souls, especially
in these places where he preached in the time of trouble.*
His son, Ebenezer, having occasion of late to be at Corn-
hill-well, found his father's name fragrant and savoury
among some old people there, who had been under his ministry, and were exceeding kind to the son for the father's
sake. He was one of undaunted boldness in his Master's
cause, and was frequently sent by the Presbytery at the

* "There are thousands yet alive," says Wodrow, speaking of this
minister in 1722, "in the places where he preached, to whom his name
and memory is most savoury, for his affectionate, close, and faithful
preaching of the gospel. As he was very bold in his Master's work, so
he was singularly blessed with remarkable success."—(History of the
Sufferings of the Church of Scotland, vol. iii. p. 404).

time of the Revolution, to preach in, and take possession
of these churches, where the body of the people were disaf-
fected to the Presbyterian interest, and where ministers
had greatest difficulty of access; and sometimes he would
have preached in these places when showers of stones would
be breaking in at the doors and widows, particularly in
Coldingham. It was somewhat observed, that the last sermon ever he preached, was to the same people who had
given him such harsh entertainment; the subject upon
which he discoursed to them being a part of Belshazzer's
sentence, (Dan. v. 27,) "Thou art weighed in the balance
and art found wanting,"* being the Monday after the administration of the sacrament of the Lord's Supper in that
place.

The manner of his death was as remarkable as his life,
being a literal accomplishment of that word, Psa. xxxvii.
37, "Mark the perfect man, and behold the upright, for
the end of that man is peace;" being seized with a fever,
of which he died in a fortnight. When he found that
death was dealing with him, having set his house in order,
he called for his children, of which there were nine alive,
and six present; and with a kind of heavenly authority he
exhorted them to cleave to the Lord with full purpose of
heart, declaring, that the advantages of religion and holiness did infinitely preponderate over all the hardships and
difficulties that possibly could attend it; and as a dying
man and a dying father, he gave his testimony to the good-

* If we may judge from a passage in Boston's Memoirs, Mr Erskine's
preaching was of an awakening kind. "According to the impressions
wherewith I was prompted to enter on trials," says Boston, "I began
my preaching of the word on a rousing strain; and would fain have set
fire to the devil's nest.   *   *   *   *   The first Sabbath I
preached, being timorous, I had not confidence to look on the people;
though I believe I did not close my eyes; yet, as a pledge of what I was
to meet with, an heritor of the parish, on that very sermon, called me
afterwards, in contempt, one of Mr Henry Erskine's disciples, in which
he spoke truth, as Caiaphas did, that worthy minister of Christ being
the first instrument of good to my soul: but the theory he meant was,
that I was a railer."—Pp. 32, 33.

ness of God's ways; and that, as he never had, so more especially now, he did not repent of any hardships he had endured in his Master's service. "I know," added he, "that I am going to heaven; and if you follow my footsteps, you and I shall have a joyful meeting there."

Having thus encouraged them to embark in the way of the Lord, he caused them, one after another, from the eldest to the youngest present, to sit down upon their knees by his bedside, and took them solemnly engaged to be servants to the God of Abraham, Isaac, and Jacob, and his God, and to keep his ways, as ever they would look him in the face at the great day of the Lord; and thereupon, like a dying Jacob, he blessed them, and recommending his wife and them to the care of divine Providence, he recommended his spirit into the hands of his covenanted God, who had cared for him all his life long.*

Sometimes he was heard say, that he desired to live no longer than to see his son Ebenezer, who was then attending the Philosophy College at Edinburgh, succeeding him in the work of his ministry. The Lord saw fit to deny him this. However, it has pleased God that he has two sons this day ministers in the Church of Scotland, viz. Ebenezer

---

* His son Ebenezer at this time was in the 16th year of his age, and Ralph only in his 11th year; but the scene of their father's last moments made a deep and solemn impression on their youthful minds, and they often recalled it to their thoughts in after life. Ebenezer refers to it in his diary in these words:—" *Portmoak, Oct.* 20, 1708.—My wife and I began to discourse about spiritual matters, and the Lord made this conversation sweet to my soul. He helped me to speak of his goodness, and to declare the riches of his grace in some measure to my soul. He made me tell how my father took engagements of me on his death-bed, and did cast me upon the providence of his God, and how the Lord had taken care of me, and never suffered me to want." Ralph, in his diary, speaking of his exercise on a day of private humiliation, observed Nov. 22, 1731, says, " I began with his mercies to me in the womb and on the breast. . . . I took special notice of *the Lord's drawing out my heart towards him at my father's death.*"—(Fraser's Memoir of Henry Erskine, prefixed to his Life of Ebenezer, p. 36; and his Life of Ralph Erskine, p. 26.)

and Ralph Erskine, the first at Portmoak, the other at Dunfermline, both within the provincial synod of Fife.

As was already said, he departed this life the 72d year of his age, August the 10th, 1696, and was buried in the Church-yard of Chirnside. Mr John Dysert, minister of Coldingham, wrote the following epitaph in Latin and English, which is engraved on his tomb, in the place foresaid to this day :

Sanctus Areskinus saxo qui conditur isto,
Est lapis æterni vivus in Æde Dei.
Non æstu lapis hic, technâve volubilis ullâ
Quippe fide, in Petra constabilitus erat.

Under this stone here lies a Stone,
Living with God above :
Built on the Rock was such a one,
Whom force nor fraud could move.

REMARKABLE PROVIDENCES AS TO MR HENRY ERSKINE. From Mr W. Veitch. Sent April 1718 by Mr Veitch.

He was a minister in the parish of ⸺ near the Scotch border, and having a numerous family, was often put to great straits. When he came to live at ⸺ in the parish of Mertoun in Teviotdale, he was frequently at my house in England, and assisted at my ordination. He told my wife and me the following things : One was, that he, his wife, and children, went to bed with a light-supper, which made the children cry in the morning, when they wakened for meat ; but there being none in the house, he bade them be still, and he would play them a spring upon the citren. He played and wept, and they and the mother wept, they being in one room, and he and his wife in bed in another. But before he had done playing, one raps at the gate, and it proved to be a servant-man sent from a worthy and charitable lady, with a horse-load of meal, cheese, and beef. Another was this: He was going one day to a meeting where he thought he might have use for money, and was walking melancholy through a piece of green ground; and looking about him, he sees somewhat clear among the grass, and when he went to lift it, it proved to be a half-crown. A third was in Edinburgh, when he took in his daughter to the school, and had nothing to pay for her education. One comes to him when he was walking melancholy in the street, and says to him, "Sir, will you walk in to this cellar and take a drink?" He was shy, being a stranger, but he urged him. While they were drinking, he told him that he had a commission from a gentleman to give him some money. "To me?" says he; "you are in a mistake, surely." "No," says the man, "it is to you." So he took out a purse, and gave him. He asked, who it was that gave him it, that he might return him thanks? He answered "Tell it, but wait until I go up stairs;" and he never came back. It was very helpful both to his daughter and family.

A fourth was in his going from Edinburgh to some week day's great meeting at Ormiston, meeting on the way with some country-people going thither, and talking to them about their great privileges of having such a minister, and such meetings freely continued to them, when others were deprived, and what a witness this would be against them if not improven. A rich countryman in the company invites him to take a drink, the kirk not being near going to, and when drinking, says to him, "Sir, God has given me abundance of the world, but I never had a heart to give any of it to good folk; but since I saw and heard you, God has opened my heart, and persuaded me you stand in need of help;" and he gave him considerably.

MEMOIR

OF

MR JOHN CARSTAIRS.

~~~~~~~~~~~~

Mr JOHN CARSTAIRS was first minister at Cathcart : then he was, very much against his will, transported to Glasgow, to be colleague to the great and excellent Mr Durham. He said to one, their taking him out of Cathcart did never go from his heart; he could never win over it, he was so desirous to stay in that small and mean congregation. Mr Peeblis told me he thought he should have killed himself with weeping; he never hardly saw any man weep so much as Mr Carstairs did, when he was transported to Glasgow.

My mother told me she heard him preach at Cathcart; and after the sermon, he did pronounce the sentence of excommunication against one Corbet, if I be not mistaken; and in the very time of his pronouncing that fearful sentence, that woeful wretch threw a stone at Mr Carstairs in the pulpit, which he very narrowly escaped.

Worthy Mr Paton of Barnweel told that he was as much edified by Mr Carstairs's first prayer as his preaching; for when he first entered on his Sabbath's work, he ordinarily prayed one hour, for he took in all the public things in that prayer; which is truly conform to our excellent Directory for Worship.

Mr M. Crawford, minister at Eastwood, told me that he

thought from the time Mr Carstairs began his first prayer
to the time of ending it, the people's faces were generally
changed.   He thought they looked with another countenance, and seemed to have another sort of frame upon them,
than they had before his prayer.

My now glorified father told me, that when worthy Mr
Andrew Gray's corpse was taking out to be buried, Mr
Carstairs was put to pray with his relict, the late Jerviswood's sister ; but, he said, such a prayer he never heard
all his life.   And I cannot but say my father used to be
very sober in his commending any person ; he never used
to speak of any thing of that kind but within the bounds
of truth and sobriety.

When they were calling Mr Carstairs to Cathcart, there
was an old minister said to a gentleman of that place, " Call
this young man, for he is a man of many meditations."

The great and learned Mr Wood, Mr Carstairs' brother-
in-law, said of Mr Carstairs, " We can some way hold up with
my brother Carstairs in lecturing or preaching, but none of
us all can hold up with him in prayer ; he there far excels
us all, and goes out of all our sight."

He was called to be with Chancellor Rothes at his death.
He had such a prayer then, in the hearing of many great
nobles, that made them all stand amazed, and be strangely
confounded ; and even a great enemy, a woman of some
note, went out of the chamber where Mr Carstairs was
praying with the Duke of Rothes, but she heard him abundantly well in the room where she was ; and was forced to
say, " I never knew the difference before so clearly, between a Prelatic and Presbyterian minister, as now I perceive, when I hear this man's prayer."   Duke Hamilton
(William Douglas) said to some of the nobles that were
with him, " This is a strange thing ! We are aye hunting
and pursuing these men in the time of our life and health ;
out we are, many of us, made to call for them at our
death !"   The Duke said to the late Orbistoun, " I never
heard such a prayer as this, since your father, Sir James

Hamilton, died." He made them all generally weep who were in the Chancellor's chamber, he had such a strange and ravishing way of prayer.

His hand, on the Sabbath, would have been all wet, as if it had been ducked, with tears, before he was done with his first prayer. In his prayer, he usually came to speak of the palm-bearing company; and in his prayer, he ordinarily used, as I hear, to have that expression and petition in many of his excellent prayers, "Oh that we may never outlive our integrity, nor die undesired!"

He was a man of great and rare piety; he was full of love; he dwelt, walked, and lived in that fire of love.

James Cowie told me, he was in a meeting wherein the Protesters and the other party were to meet to make up some agreement. Some of the protesting ministers said, they would agree with their brethren, if they would confess some faults they were guilty of. Mr Carstairs said, "Let us agree with our brethren, though they should never confess a fault." The worthy Mr Rutherford said, "Oh! but that brother has much of heaven in his bosom, for he lives, dwells, and walks in love. But I cannot say so of several other ministers in some Presbyteries of this Church, that will not suffer some excellent and worthy young men pass trials, merely because they are not for the Public Resolutions."

I have heard my father, or some who heard him, tell that he was visiting Mr Carstairs some time after he was turned out of his charge; and Mr Carstairs said to him, "Brother, I cannot but say, though the nobles of our land have deprived us of our stipends and maintenance, yet all this time bygone our stipends have been right well paid to us by the Lord himself."

He was an excellent and brave orator, and of a most tender and melting frame and disposition; for he used to weep much in prayer, and I know not but he weeped also much in preaching; also, even in ordinary discourse, he spake like an orator, and above the ordinary way of speaking. He was nobly well-bred, and well-behaved towards every person he had to do with. He was very neat in wearing his clothes. Ye would have known him to be a well-born gentleman by his courteous carriage, as indeed he was. He would have penned a letter notably well to great and mean persons.

I heard a very strange passage anent him; that Mr Thomas Melville, at Calder, did give him a call to come and assist him at a communion. When he came to preach, Mr Melville happened to be sick and unwell, that he could not go out and preach the action-sermon, and so laid it on Mr Carstairs; and he did preach it, and was well assisted therein; and when he came to consecrate the elements, he was more than ordinarily assisted, and did serve the tables so well, that though there were several worthy honest ministers there, none of them would so much as come near, and serve any of the tables. Mr Carstairs was in a kind of holy rapture all the time, and was necessitate to serve all the tables himself. I know not whether there were ten, twelve, or sixteen. When he ended, after the action-sermon, he caused sing the 24th Psalm, 7th verse, and James Gray, that worthy elder in Calder, said, that he hardly ever saw so much of the glory of God shine forth and evidently appear as did that day in that kirk, in singing that psalm there was; and there was even a sort of glory shining, and evidently appearing among the people, without the church, in the churchyard; that some without the church cried out, "Oh! what a glory appears here?" They would have gladly been within the church, that they might have seen the great glory that behoved to be there. "What glory," said they, "must be within, when so much appears without, visibly!"

His body at that time got a sore stress, for when some were seeking him to assist at some other communion, he told them that his body was really brought low by what he was made to do at Calder.

I heard another strange passage, which I wish I could get well attested. It was either at Kirkintilloch or Kilsyth. The communion tables were all ended, and the evening sermon after the tables was fully ended, and when the people were just ready to go home, it being far in the evening, there comes on immediately a most fearful and terrible shower of rain, that forced the people to stay, a great part of them, within the church for a considerable time. Mr Carstairs being there, and seeing the people fall to their idle and vain discoursing one with another, he, to divert them from that, goes up to the pulpit, and has an excellent extemporary discourse to them about faith in Christ, persuading them earnestly to close with him. And it was said to me, if I be not forgotten, that by that extemporary discourse of Mr Carstairs, there should have been about two hundred or three hundred persons converted, among whom James Gray himself was one. Cartsburn told me, he had this passage from the late James Gray, who was sent away in the late bad times to America to be sold as a slave, and yet he was most favourably dealt with among these strangers, and met with kindness, and came home, and was very instrumental in getting Calder planted by Mr Ramsay, my brother-in-law, who had also a call to Campsie and Old Kilpatrick at the same time.

This James Gray's wife, a worthy Christian, told her husband, when he was sent away to be sold as a slave in America, that he would come back again to Scotland, and she herself would see him again at Christon, his own house, in Calder parish; for she had gotten the faith of it, as she said, and nothing would make her believe the contrary; which accordingly fell out. His wife was sister to that worthy Christian and elder, Thomas Pettigrew, in the Green of the Westerton of Shettleston, in the Barony parish of Glasgow.

Mr Carstairs was most tender and exact in his practice. He was very averse from ministers meddling with any work but what properly belonged to them.

When his son, Mr William Carstairs, was put to suffer for meddling with these grievances in Lauderdale's time, that I suppose Sir James Stewart, the late advocate, had drawn up, and his son Mr William was released after some time's imprisonment, I did hear that his father, Mr John Carstairs, did solemnly charge him never to meddle with such things again, but to exercise himself in preaching and prayer, and what other exercises did properly belong to a faithful minister of the gospel: and it was most grievous to that worthy man, when his son fell into that same evil that he had formerly discharged him to meddle with; for which he was made to suffer sadly in the year 1684, about the time of his worthy father's death; and his father was so angry at him, that he would not for several days suffer his son to come near him, for he had most evidently disobeyed his worthy father's commands.

And this confirms to me what the late Sir William Stewart of Castlemilk told me at Castleton. He went with his mother, the late worthy Lady Castlemilk, to visit Mr Carstairs at his own house at Edinburgh. She caused her son Sir William to go out of the chamber where Mr Carstairs was, till she discoursed a little with Mr John Carstairs. He went out, but not being very far from the chamber, he heard Mr Carstairs say, "Madam, I have a son called Mr William, and a good-son, Mr William Dunlop; they will be aye plotting and plodding till they plod the heads off themselves; and this is very grievous to me, for as they are ministers of the gospel, they are not called to meddle with that work which noblemen and gentlemen may very lawfully be called to." This Sir William told me.

I do very well remember I did hear, when worthy Mr Carstairs died, which was some time before the happy and glorious Revolution, and on the same day with the excellent Mr Melville, minister at Calder, who died at Drumry in East Kilpatrick, he should have called his daughter, Mrs Dunlop, and given her a solemn charge, which he ordered her to give both to her husband and her brother, Mr William Carstairs, that so they never meddled with any work but what properly belonged to them as ministers of the gospel.

When he was dying, he had these expressions: "I am dying, and dying in the Lord; and now I have nothing to do but to die." He called all his children, and blessed them; and he added, " Yea, and they shall be blessed."

And yet this was the man that was the chief butt of Archbishop Sharp's malice and fury; for he persecuted him most of any, because of his being witness to famous Mr James Wood's testimony, which he gave at his death to Presbyterian Government, as is set down in Naphthali.

When several of the honest ministers were one day together, and pretty cheerful and merry, and they were inquiring at one another, What they would be, and what they would turn themselves to, when they could not get their ministry followed? One said, he would be this, and another that; and honest Mr Carstairs says, very gravely, " I think I could be a laird." At which all the company smiled and laughed very heartily.

It was Mr Carstairs that gave the late Mr Robert Alexander, one of the principal clerks of the Session, right and true impressions of the late renowned and worthy Marquis of Argyle. When Mr Carstairs spoke of that nobleman, Mr Alexander told me he usually called him " that noble Prince in our land!" Mr Alexander had met with some malignant persons who had been at great pains to misrepresent that worthy nobleman to him; and so was under very bad impressions of him, till he met Mr Carstairs, who did very clearly and fully acquit the Marquis of all these base calumnies they had endeavoured to fasten on him.

Mr Carstairs was called to be with the Marquis, to preach to him in the prison on the last Sabbath of his life. The Marquis saw one of the bailies come in to hear; whereupon the Marquis spoke a little in secret to Mr Carstairs, before he began to preach, that Mr Carstairs might be in an especial manner on his guard, in his preaching or prayer, to utter nothing anent the severity of that sentence now passed upon him; " for I suppose," said the Marquis, " this bailie is sent in by our rulers to be a spy, to take away anything he can hear that may serve in the least to reflect on the present Government."

Worthy Mr Carstairs was taken among the dead at Dunbar, and stripped naked, and lay for some time among the dead ; and he said there came some soldier to strip the dead bodies of men of what could be useful to them, and he came upon him, and set his foot upon him near about his lisk ;* but he said he never bore a greater stress than that was, for he behoved not to stir, lest he should have been slain immediately, for they thought he had been dead. There came at length a poor woman to him, and inquired at him, If he desired any thing of her ? He said to her "If ye could give me a napkin I would desire it ;" for he was weeping sore. He inquired at her, If she saw Mr James Guthrie ride by her ? for he was much concerned about his safety.

When he was brought before the Council, at the time when many were denying the king's authority, a little before King Charles II. died, they inquired at Mr Carstairs, If he acknowledged the king's authority ? He answered, Take away Mr Paterson,—who was then Archbishop of Glasgow, —he did own the authority of all the rest that were present. The late Lord Ross said to my father, they were all very well satisfied with Mr Carstairs' discourse that he had before the Council ; and that he was not pleased that Archbishop Paterson should have meddled with him, for Mr Carstairs, according to his own principles, could not speak otherwise.

He was much troubled with the gout for a long time, and I suppose it came upon his heart, and killed him.

When he was in his hiding, in his Patmos, he made some pleasant verses, which I have seen in print. Mr Carstairs died at Edinburgh, February 5. 1686, in the morning ; and Mr Thomas Melville, minister of Calder, died at Drumry, February 5. 1686, at night.

* Groin.

EDINBURGH. PRINTED BY JOHN GREIG

CPSIA information can be obtained at www.ICGtesting.com
Printed in the USA
LVOW111841270612

287935LV00012B/66/P